KT-166-587

Allan Morrison is the author of 13 books with sales well in advance of a quarter of a million copies. Media appearances include Richard and Judy, The One Show and the Fred McAuley Show. Allan is a Rotarian and a very popular after-dinner speaker. Now retired, he enjoys raising funds for local charities and bagging Munros. He lives in the west of Scotland with his wife.

AH COULDNAE BELIEVE MA EARS!

A hilarious collection of overheard banter

Allan Morrison

hachette
SCOTLAND

First published in 2009 by
HACHETTE SCOTLAND, an imprint of
HACHETTE UK

9

Cataloguing in Publication Data is available from the British Library

ISBN 978 0 7553 1949 7

Illustrations © Rupert Besley

Designed and typeset by Susie Bell

Printed and bound in Great Britain by Clays Ltd, St Ives Plc

Hachette Scotland's policy is to use papers that are natural, renewable and recyclable products and made from wood grown in sustainable forests. The logging and manufacturing processes are expected to conform to the environmental regulations of the country of origin.

HACHETTE SCOTLAND
An Hachette UK Company
338 Euston Road
London NW1 3BH

www.hachettescotland.co.uk
www.hachette.co.uk

CONTENTS

Dedicated to all the people who passed on the funny conversations they overheard, plus the folks who actually uttered them!

INTRODUCTION

Scotland is a country of unquenchable exuberance, bubbling enthusiasm… and conversation.

People from other lands think the Scots are rugged folks who live on mountains and have a daily diet of porridge, mince or haggis, all washed down with Irn-Bru and whisky; that we weave tartan and wear kilts, play a strange, tormenting instrument, are friendly and hospitable and love golf but keep our pennies tucked safely in weird, hairy purses.

Some of this may be true, but what is indubitably factual is that we are a nation of blethers. Our favourite pastime is having a natter. Once in a Canadian airport I was looking for the check-in desk for my flight to Scotland. I didn't need to look at the information board as I could hear the queue from two hundred yards away.

Indeed someone once said that Scotland is the only place in the world where you can stand at a bus stop, then get on the bus, go to the shops, have a cup of tea and when you get home write a book about everything you have overheard.

This is that book, capturing life as it is in Scotland today.

Not only do we like to chat but we are very nosey. And who

would argue that there is nothing more entertaining than accidentally, or otherwise, overhearing a snippet of conversation containing a choice nugget of information? Sometimes you are able to block out the extemporaneous noise of your surroundings, but then you suddenly catch an interesting word. Well, you're immediately up for it; all ears.

Imagine you are sitting on the bus or train, eyes closed after a day's work or shopping, when nearby a couple of voices strike up. You surreptitiously listen. 'Aye, she says that she is goin' tae leave him if he doesnae stop "you know what".' Well, you've just got to listen, haven't you? People have been known to go past their stop just to find out the ending to such free entertainment. Or someone gets on their mobile phone and you find yourself party to one side of a fascinating conversation.

Ah Couldnae Believe Ma Ears! demonstrates this blethering with its mixture of outspoken, humorous talk and opinionated comment. It is a treasure trove of outrageous gems and verbal banana skins. Some of the dialogue, with its unconscious humour and colourful viewpoints, is the stuff of the man in the street and his wee woman. They will happily share their 'less than humble' opinions on every subject imaginable, wrestle with the enigma of life's mysteries, and deliver their thoughts with the swagger and confidence of an expert. And of course this country has thrown up more than its fair share of mental giants. No doubt their inspiration also started with a good blether.

The use of the vernacular raises its head in many

conversations. Indeed, pungent words tell you something about the nation. Mild insults, such as heidbanger, eejit and numptie are heard frequently when eavesdropping.

In Scotland you can always be entertained sitting or standing near people chatting. It doesn't seem to matter how busy people are, they are never too busy to stop and talk, even if all it's about is how busy they are. And it is amazing that so many folks seem delightfully unconcerned that their outlandish private conversations are being overheard. Information is passed on sometimes with a laugh, occasionally with a tear or a wink, but usually with open-eyed sincerity.

And the beauty is you get a new show, morning, noon and night.

Apart from listening in to dialogues myself and getting a few odd glances in return, I asked all friends and an army of acquaintances to be on the lookout for interesting chit-chat. Christmas, birthday and greetings cards all had a slip enclosed requesting suitable input. I am therefore indebted to the many people who passed on overheard palavers to make this book possible.

OVERHEARD ON THE STREETS

Overheard in Cumbernauld. Two-year-old girl dragging her dolly along the pavement.
'Veronica! Carry that wean or the Social will come an' take it intae care!'

Overheard in Pollok, Glasgow.
'Ah go to that Friendship Club doon in the church hall. We meet every Wednesday afternoon. Ye get a nice wee cup o' tea and a blether.'
'Friendship Club! Ah know at least two o' them auld biddies that go to that club, and ah wid be feart tae go up a dark street wi' either o' them.'

Overheard in Pittenweem.
'D'you ken whit I'm saying, Ken?'

Overheard in Glasgow city centre.

'Was my father a hoarder? Listen, when I was emptying his house I came across a jar with a label on it which read, "Contents: string – too short to be of any further use".'

Overheard in Newton Mearns.

'I couldn't believe it. He opened four spades. There was me sitting with three of them.'

'What did the opposition bid?'

'Well, that was remarkable. They bid five clubs. I was utterly confused, so I doubled.'

'What was the final contract?'

'This chap I was partnering actually went five spades and got it. He had a heart attack when he got home and ended up in hospital. Apparently he'll survive. I fancy him as my partner next month. In fact ... I fancy him as my partner!'

Overheard in Aberdeen city centre.

'But the specialist was quite specific, Mary.'

'Don't be stupid. How could a seventy-two-year-old man have gonorrhoea?'

'Well, if Mum was alive she'd die wi' embarrassment.'

Conversation between two men meeting in the street in Stirling.

'Hi.'

'Better day.'

'Freeze yer chookies.'
'Nae rain.'
'Wull it last?'
'Nae tellin''
'See ye.'

Overheard in Buchanan Street, Glasgow.
'See that Hadron Collider thingmibob that cost millions in some circular tunnel. They could have used the Glesca Underground an' saved a fortune.'

Overheard in Airdrie.
'There's only the two o' us left in the hoose noo. The children are all down south with partners and weans. So it's just me an' him. That's why ah like tae dae aw the talkin' masel'. It saves time and prevents arguments, ah always say.'

Overheard in Castle Street, Glasgow, on a Saturday afternoon.

'You and me is finished. Finished! Dae ye hear me?'

'But ah love you, ma wee pet.'

'Don't "wee pet" me! You say ye love me. Aye, you love half the women in Glesca and love drinking in half the pubs. You're just a big pain in the arse, so ye ur!'

'Okay then. Why don't we get merrit.'

'Ur ye serious?'

'Aye.'

'Oh, ah cannae wait tae tell ma mammy.'

Beggar in St Enoch's Car Park, Glasgow.

'Gonnae gie us two pound fifty-nine pence fur a pair o' gloves, darlin'? Ma haunds are freezin'.'

'Two pounds fifty-nine pence. Why such an exact amount?'

'Listen, hen, ah've allowed fur the reduction in VAT.'

Overheard in Edinburgh.

'He's very fit. Spends half-an-hour doing a workout every morning before he goes to the office.'

'Well, if he would muscle in and do half-an-hour's work in the office every day, he might get fit for promotion.'

Overheard in East Kilbride town centre.

'Excuse me, hen, but could ...'

'Listen, ah'm no' a hen. Dae ye see ony chicken wings or

turkey necks oan me?'
'Very sorry, ah didnae mean tae upset ye, hen.'

Overheard in Buchanan Street, Glasgow.
Two assistants smoking outside a shop.
'Bitter the day, sure it is?'
'Freezin'. Good job we put on oor coats. Got tae look efter yer health, ah say.'
'Aye, so ye dae.'

Overheard in Paisley.
'A woman in Marks came up to me and said did I know I was only wearing one earring. And so I was. So, I took the other one off and put it in a bin. It was only cheap rubbish I got out of a charity shop. Then when I got home I found the other one in my pocket. See me, ah'm no' right, ye know.'

Overheard in Helensburgh.
'Sorry, George, but ah cannae go oot on Saturday night. Broke, cards up tae their limit. A casualty of finance is me.'
'Well, ye'll jist need tae stay in an' watch Casualty instead, then.'

Overheard in Leith.
'Did you see that new coat she had on? Probably cost a fortune. She must have won the lottery.'
'Naw, it's a cheepie. Three numbers would get you that.'

Overheard in Motherwell.
'He was sitting there reading his Para Handy book. He saw me looking at him. He looked up and said, "Sorry pet, but ma Vital Spark has sunk." I had to laugh.'

Overheard in Pitlochry.
'I get bouts of forgetfulness, too. The trouble is it's usually halfway up the stairs and I don't know whether to go up or down.'

Overheard in Edinburgh.
'I'm fair yukkared.'
'Never heard that word afore, mate.'
'I just made it up. I was eating a yoghurt and it wis yukky, past its sell-by date.'
'Did ye eat the hale thing?'
'I didnae realise it wis aff. Thought it wis a new flavour.'

Overheard in a Falkirk street.
'Sure it's the simple pleasures in life that are the best, sure it is.'
'Ye're right. And see ma Harry, he must be aboot the simplest o' them all.'

Overheard in Paisley.
'Ah saw ma husband's old girlfriend the other day. Oooh, ah jist loved it. She's twice as fat as ah am, you know!'

Overheard in Falkirk.
'Yes, last week I met your daughter in Tesco.'
'I don't have a daughter. That would be my older sister.'
'Oh, sorry.'

Overheard in street in Musselburgh.
'Is he still oan the bevvie?'
'Aye, cannae get him aff the drink. Probably kill him. Sobering thought, sure it is?'

Overheard in Stevenston, Ayrshire.
'Half the folk in this town are oan sticks, half are oan mobiles, an' the other half are oan benefits.'

Overheard in street in Irvine.
'It really upsets me when people have a dig at his hair or his looks. Maybe I'm a bit sensitive, way too defensive. We've been

together now for years. I take care of him and he takes care of me. And he just loves cuddles.'

'So, where is he today?'

'He's in Ayr at the vet having his claws clipped.'

Overheard in Glasgow.

'See ma auld parents, always arguing, so they are. Gets on ma wick so it does. Like two bad-tempered toddlers after a day at the nursery. An' they're going a bit doo-lally. Ah don't know whether to laugh or cry.'

Overheard in Lenzie.

'We used to go to Millport when I was young. I can remember those donkey rides on the sand. Then eating whelks wi' pins. Magic. It's a shame everybody goes tae Spain nooadays.'

'You're right. So where are you off to next?'

'Well, we are hoping to go to Benidorm soon.'

Overheard in Hamilton.

'The tears were running down ma cheeks last night. It wis a

scream. Nane o' this modern day rubbish wi' swearing and dirty stuff. It wis the Morecambe and Wise Christmas Show from nineteen-seventy-seven.'

'But this is June. It's not Christmas.'

'Aye, but ye're allowed tae laugh at ony time o' the year. Nae law against it.'

Overheard in Edinburgh.

'I just wish I had a waist.'

'Do you not have one?'

'I lost mine when the children came and I've never found it again. Must be in a lost property office somewhere.'

Overheard in George Square outside the City Chambers. American tourist to driver polishing Council limousine which has a distinctive number plate, 'GO'.

'Gee, who does this lovely automobile belong to?'

'The Lord Provost, madam.'

'And is the Lord Provost a very important person in Glasgow?'

'Aye, madam.'

'And what does the GO stand for?'

'Aw naw, the D's fell aff!'

Overheard in Anderston, Glasgow, as man and woman get out of a car.

'You didnae put on that tie ah wanted ye tae wear. Now, remember, nane o' yer dirty jokes. This wee couple's nice.'

Overheard in Queen Street, Glasgow.
'Wid ye have any spare change, pal?'
'Aye, ah dae. Cheerio.'

Overheard in Falkirk.
'You can get yer pension paid weekly, you know. You've got to enquire so you have to. Government bumph is only good fur usin' as bumph, ah say.'

Overheard in St Andrews.
'After being married for eighteen years ah feel the best years are yet tae come.'
'So are ye finally going tae gie him the punt, then?'

Overheard in Sauchiehall Street. Husband dropping off wife and shouting to her as he drives away.
'Now, get on wi' the soliciting. We need the money! There's a credit crunch, you know.'
'Charles! You're impossible.'

Overheard in George Street, Edinburgh.
'Ah'm starving. Whit's it gonnae be for lunch? Burger King, eh?'
'How about just a cup of herbal tea, dear. You know how I'm

trying to diet and it's the slimming club tonight.'
'So I've to go around all afternoon with ma belly rumbling, eh?
Let's compromise and find a McDonald's.'
'OK. But I'll just have a cup of tea, dear.
Maybe a burger, too.
Oh, stuff this dieting business.'

Overheard outside a tenement close in
Glasgow.
'Sorry if ma cat scratched you.
She's usually very good.
There must be something
wrong with her.'
'There's nothing wrong wi'
that cat that a Hong Kong
chef couldnae fix.'

Overheard in George Square,
Glasgow.
'I've started writing my Christmas cards. I was late last year,
especially with the ones for the family in the States. But see wi'
the price of stamps, noo, I would be cheaper capturing wan of
those pigeons over there.'

Overheard in Aberdeen.
'Naw, when it's time fur me to go into a care home ah'm goin''

intae that new wan up the road. Ah hear they've goat good-lookin' male nurses that take yer knickers aff fur ye.'

Overheard in street in Calton, Glasgow.
'Are you alright, missus?'
'Ah'm no' drunk, son, if that's whit ye think. Ah'm wearin' ma sister's shoes while she's in Spain. She comes back next Sunday.'

Overheard in Edinburgh.
'Ah wish ah wis a bit taller. Boys don't really fancy wee females. Ah don't know whit tae dae aboot it.'
'Listen, you're only fourteen. You'll get a lot taller over the next couple o' years.'
'Ah hope so. If you're taller it's easier tae snog.'

Overheard in Dundee.
'He made it clear right from the start that he fancied me. We went out a few times an' it wis going great, then he stopped texting me. I think his mate wisnae too keen on the fact that I've got the wean. I think this is out of order. Dae ye no' think?'
'Ye're right, Samantha. Ah mean, you're a great parent tae wee Georgie.'

'Ah um. Even went tae bed wi' that toerag. Lousy he wis, tae. Been wi' thousands o' guys better than him.'

Overheard in Glasgow.
'He says he thought the doors opened automatically and he banged his head on the glass. It didn't break or anything, but he came up all black and blue. Now he tells everybody he was practising his Glesca Kiss!'

Overheard on pavement in Princes Street in Edinburgh.
'The wife's got a terrible cold. She should really be in her bed. And noo she's lost her voice. I don't know what I can do to help her.'
'Easy. Just come in at four in the morning stupit drunk.'

Overheard on Rothesay promenade.
'I bet if you heard some of the things women say about men it would make your hair curl.'
'That would take a bit o' doing wi' ma bald pate.'

Overheard in East Kilbride. Two ladies smoking outside office building.
'Ah thought ye said ye wurnae going oot wi' him again? Ye said he had dirty underwear.'

OVERHEARD ON THE MOBILE

Overheard in optician's in Edinburgh. Assistant on mobile while customers get impatient.
'Ah jist loved being wi' you last night. Mind you, you're apt tae take a girl like me fur granted. Haud on a minute, wid ye, ah think ma husband's trying tae get through on the phone here.'

Overheard mobile conversation in Cumbernauld.
'Ah've only got one pound left in this thing, so talk fast.'
'__'
'Ah'm no good at texting. Sure ah told ye that.'
'__'
'Look, stop the lecture. Just talk or ah'm offski tae the rub-a-dub-dub.'

Overheard mobile in Glasgow.
'Did a flyer doon the stairs so he did. Whit a scream. Best laugh ah've had since Granny caught her tits in the mangle.'

Overheard mobile
conversation in Paisley.
'Hey, you've asked me fur ma account number, the first and
fourth letters o' ma password, and noo ma postcode. Wid it no'
just be a good idea tae ask me whit ma name is?'

Young woman on mobile in car park in Edinburgh city centre.
'Aye, she's thingamy.'
'__'
'Aye, thingamy.'
'__'
'You know, thingamy.'
'__'
'That's whit ah said, "thingamy".'

Overheard on Princes Street, Edinburgh. Beggar on mobile.
'And another thing, ah told ye no' tae call me when ah'm at
the office!'

Overheard in Tesco, Port Glasgow. Woman on mobile in food section.
'Never heard o' him. Whit's he like?'
'__'
'Is he separated or divorced?'
'__'
'He's hung like a whit?!'
'__'

'Naw, don't fancy him. Anyways, how dae you know about his gentles?'

Overheard on mobile in Asda, Linwood.
'You said you wanted the larger size with buttons at the back, but they don't have any.'
'—'
'Of course ah asked an assistant. Dae ye think ma heid is buttoned up the back, tae?'

Overheard mobile conversation in Gallowgate, Glasgow.
'Aye, it's a personality cult nooadays, sure it is. Aw they tuppence-halfpenny celebrities that naebuddy has ever heard o'. See that I'm a Celebrity Get Me Out Of Here!? Rubbish it is. Ye wouldnae have got the likes o' Harry Lauder and Jimmy Logan doing that.'

Overheard in café in Sauchiehall Street, Glasgow. Young lady on mobile.
'Ah couldnae wait to tell Jenny in the office. It wis the best fifteen minutes o' ma life, so it wis. See when he put his hand … Never mind, I'll give ye the details later.'

Overheard in Queen Street Station, Glasgow. Woman on mobile.
'It's me, Sadie. Ah wis jist phoning tae see whit his sentence wis. Did he get Community Service?'
'—'
'Oh, an' whit's yer name, then?'

'—'

'Sorry, wrang number!'

Overheard on train to Ayr. Man on mobile.
'I'm on the train.'
'—'

'I said I'm on the train.'
'—'

'I'm on the TRAIN!'
'—'

'Och, for heavens sake put a shilling in the meter! See you when I get home.'

Overheard mobile call outside Queen Street Station, Glasgow.
'I know they say that it's better to give than receive, but the only thing you've ever given me is the cold!'

Overheard on mobile at Prestwick Airport.
'Never says anything clever, that eejit. Ah think his wife just learns him a couple o' words every time he goes oot, just so he can pass himsel'.'

Overheard mobile conversation on platform of Waverley Station, Edinburgh.
'For sheer brass neck you take the biscuit. Ah've got tae admire your cheek. Ye never admit doing anything wrang. Contrition is

a word unknown to you.'

'_'

'Contrition was the word ah said.'

'_'

'You're ignorant.'

'_'

'You're worse than him.'

'_'

'Ah'm entitled tae ma opinion and it's better than yours.'

'_'

'And you!'

Overheard mobile call at bus stop in Motherwell.
'So ah said, och, away, ah don't believe it. And she said, nae kiddin'. An' ah said, naw definitely. So she said, ye're oan. So that's you up tae date wi things. Alright? Here's ma bus. Cheerio.'

Overheard mobile conversation in Clydesdale Bank in Edinburgh.
'Get your clothes on. Ye cannae walk aboot like that.'

'_'

'Are you just hell bent on entertaining the neighbours?'

'_'

'Aye, that's better. Tattie bye!'

Overheard on Helensburgh train from Glasgow. Young woman on mobile.
'No, he is at work just now.'

'___'

'Fine, fine.'

'___'

'He's working overtime tonight. I'll not see him till about ten.'

'___'

'Ah don't know where he gets the energy. Ma body feels as though it's been through a wringer every night. Anyway, must go. Cheerio, Mum.'

Overheard mobile conversation on the Edinburgh to Glasgow train.
'It's me again. I was just thinking, you'll need to tell him a wee lie.'

'___'

'Well, it'll cost me a lot of money if you don't.'

'___'

'Hey, it's my money. Remember that.'

'___'

'Do that and you'll never hear from me again.'

Overheard mobile conversation at Clydebank bus stop.
'Listen, genius. How did ye come up wi that wan?'

'___'

'At least we'll never see you on Mastermind.'

'___'

'Naw.'

'___'

'Naw.'

'_'

'Naw.'

'_'

'Cheerio, ma wee Brain o' Britain.'

Overheard in foyer of Royal Concert Hall in Glasgow. Man on mobile.

'Hello Jane, it's Roger. How are you?'

'_'

'Sorry to hear that. When did it swell up?'

'_'

'What did the specialist say?'

'_'

'You'll need to take things easy.'

'_'

'Sorry, I can't come over tonight. I'm in Aberdeen right now.'

OVERHEARD ON THE TOURIST TRAIL

Overheard as a group of tourists were getting off a tour bus near the Scottish Parliament in Edinburgh. Question to driver.

'What exactly is the purpose of the Scottish Parliament building?'

'Now, that's a very good question.'

Overheard at the top of the Devil's Staircase on the West Highland Way. Walker patting his dog.

'Four days ago I said "walkies" to him, and that's about seventy-five miles so far. The next time he hears "walkies" I bet he'll not move.'

Overheard at Edinburgh Castle.

'If you ask me he is a bit o' a "jack-the-lad". Aye, gearing up for his next conquest. There's not a woman safe this side o' the Mississippi!'

Overheard in Aviemore Centre.

'Why is there no Scottish entry for the Eurovision, that's what I want to know? Why has it always got to be a British entry?

I mean we have great Scottish songs.'
'Such as?'
'What's the matter with Donald, Whaur's Yer Troosers?'

Overheard as large party of Scots on a bus tour are being escorted round a Highland castle by the titled owner. 'Actually, ladies and gentlemen, in the nineteenth century my great-great-great grandmother was one of the kitchen maids. So you see, ladies and gentlemen, I'm probably a bastard.'
Loud whisper from the back of the group. 'Aye, a jammy bastard!'

Overheard on a Highland ferry.
'She's aye goat her hemline up o'er her knees. Och, there's not a man safe within a hundred yards.'
'Ye're right. She's the sexiest woman ah know wi' a zimmer.'

Overheard in Fort William.
'See this cardigan. I bought it when I was doon in Glesca a few years ago. It's a bit chunky knit but since I lost aw that weight it doesnae really show ma boobs noo.'

Overheard at Glencoe Village.
'I was a bit disappointed when we went up north. I mean, I expected to see little old ladies sitting at spinning wheels and things like that.'
'Nooadays ye wid need tae go tae the bingo tae see that.'

Overheard just outside Fort William.
'Excuse me, where is Ben Nevis?'
'Just raise yer eyes over tae the left. Ye cannae see it. It's playing hide and seek under that big cloud.'

Overheard at Cairngorm Ski Centre booking office. Spanish visitor talking to helpful assistant.
'Please, I wish wee ski.'
'I could recommend a couple of malts you could get down in Aviemore, sir.'

Overheard in Islay.
'Do you understand the Gaelic on the telly, then?'
'Only when they have subtitles.'

Overheard on a Cally Mac boat approaching Oban.
'De 'n uair a tha e ann?'
'Sorry, mate. I'm from Oz.'

Overheard at the pier on a certain Hebridean island. Ferryman instructing visitor.
'Dinnae gie me the money. Ah'll jist drink it. Gie it intae the tea room.'

Tourist talking to seaman on the ferry.
'Should malt whisky be drunk neat?'
'You can drink it wearing a collar and tie if you like, just as long as you don't put Irn-Bru in it.'

Overheard outside a café in Callander. Tourist talking to local.
'Is it raining?'
'Naw.'
'Then why am I getting wet?'
'That's Scotch mist.'

OVERHEARD DURING SPORTING EVENTS

Overheard at football match in Edinburgh.
'It disnae matter whit ah say, she's aye got a different viewpoint frae mine. Ah jist cannae win.'
'Ye're right. Women should come wi' a set o' instructions.'
'Aye, an' from bitter experience the first instruction should be never to laugh at their clothes. Otherwise they're out there spending a fortune on new ones.'

Overheard on bowling green in Dumbarton.
'Dae ye ever see Charlie?'
'Aye, wance in a while ah see him aw the time.'

Overheard at Junior football match in Glasgow.
'The papers said that before he took over this lot, at wan time he worked in a fishmongers.'
'Ah hope he's got a cure fur this bunch o' haddies.'

Overheard in hospitality suite at Cappielow Park, Greenock.
'Did ye see that the German football team, Borussia Dortmund, have a special cemetery just for their football supporters? It's

called "After the final whistle".'
'Well, I can think of a few Scottish clubs where they should bury the team and keep the supporters!'

Overheard at Firhill Stadium, Glasgow.
'That Andy Murray's been dae'n well. He must be slowly building up a fortune.'
'Aye, he's minted, so he is. Like Murray Mints, "the too good tae hurry mints".'

Overheard at Ibrox Stadium, Glasgow.
'Why don't they play proper wingers any more? Wee Willie Henderson would have run circles roon that left back.'
'Naw, noo. He's probably oan two sticks an' a pension.'

Overheard at Tynecastle Stadium, Edinburgh.
'He started to go to Gamblers' Anonymous and it helped. He used to lose hundreds on the gee-gees but his wife is now keeping a tight rein on the money.'

Overheard at Hampden Park, Glasgow. Spectator commenting on one of the team managers.

'Ye can even tell frae up here, he's either had a facelift or taken up modelling at an embalmer's night class.'

Overheard at Ibrox Stadium.

'Our neighbour is a season ticket holder at Parkhead. He's got a new dog and he's called it Celtic.'

'Well, ah hope he doesnae feed it Winalot!'

Schools football match being played at Parklea Pitch, Langbank. Left back blootered the ball, which hit the top of a train then bounced back on to the pitch. The referee was amazed.

'Do you do trick shots, son?

'Aye, but only when ah know the train oot o' Woodhall is due.'

Overheard at Tannadice Park, Dundee.

'He is very good at going past players until he gets into the box. Then he goes all to pieces. They should call him Jigsaw.'

Overheard at Hampden Park.

'Did you see that bit in the paper that the number of alcoholics in Scotland would fill every football stadium? Personally ah'm no' surprised at that statistic. For instance, take the game the day. The standard o' football in Scotland would drive anybuddy tae drink.'

Overheard at rugby international at Murrayfield.

'My wife gets very nervous in the car, especially on the motorways. She's developing into a backseat driver.'

'Tell me about it. My wife's the same. It's got to the stage where she really does all the driving and I just sit there holding the wheel waiting for the next instruction.'

Overheard at football match on playing fields in Paisley.

'See that defence, their combined talents could fit intae baith a flea's navel an' a bumblebee's erse.'

Overheard at Ibrox Stadium.

'They say that the reserve team is now full o' first-team players.'

'If you ask me, they are scraping the tap o' the barrel.'

Overheard at rugby match in Edinburgh.

'Never reacts when I try to chat to her. She might be a real dish but I find her a cold fish.'

'Looks as though you've had your chips, then.'

Overheard at Ibrox Stadium.
'The game is on Sky today and I've asked the wife to record it. Ah just hope the cameras don't pick me out eating this pie. The doctor told me ah wisnae to clog up ma plumbing.'

Overheard at Cappielow Park, Greenock.
'That sweeper couldnae sweep up anything. And he cannae tackle either. Useless.'
'Couldnae tackle a fish supper, him. And see the manager's team selection the day; that man couldnae pick his nose.'

Overheard at Firhill Stadium.
'I heard he told someone that he was the eighth child in his family, and if his mother and father had used contraceptives Partick Thistle wouldnae have had a decent forward.'

Overheard at Cappielow Park.
'Hey, ref, ur ye blind in baith ears?'

Overheard at bowling club AGM, Glasgow.
'Right, so it is agreed, gentlemen, that the Standing Committee should now sit down?'

Overheard at Celtic Park.

'Never leave a Celtic match early. They fairly keep ye on edge, but the Tic are good at scoring at the death.'

'We had a guy die on the bus on the way back fae the game a fortnight ago. At least he saw the hale match afore he went.'

Overheard outside Hampden Park at a football international. Glasgow drunk to policeman on horse. It is pouring with rain and the policeman is wearing an extended cape covering most of the horse.

'Hey Big Man! Did ye know ye've goat a horse stickin' oot yer jaiket?'

OVERHEARD AT THE SHOPS

Overheard in Post Office in Stirling.

'How's your girl doing?'

'Great. She's got a boyfriend, you know. Donald is his name. Lovely hair and teeth. Always well dressed and speaks ever so well. Nice wee lad.'

'That's awfa nice. How old is she now?'

'Three next March.'

Overheard in Silverburn Shopping Centre, Glasgow.

'Ah think him o'er there is an MSP. He was on the news wan night. Go and ask him.'

'Don't be daft.'

'If ye did speak tae him, whit would you say tae him?'

'Tell us wan o' yer wee lies.'

'Don't you dare! Ah wid be black affronted.'

Overheard at entrance to Silverburn Shopping Centre.

'Excuse me, sir. Could I interest you in insulating your loft? It would probably save you in excess of one hundred and fifty pounds each year. It could also make your home much cosier,

especially in the winter.'
'Nae good tae me, mate. I'll be in the jile next week.'

Overheard in Braehead shopping complex.
'Ah see he had on his pained look the day. And where did that
walking stick and limp come from?'
'Must be going doon tae the Social tae see them aboot his benefits.'

Overheard in a Farmfoods shop, Greenock.
'Do you sell Smiley Faces?'
'Sorry, they're sold oot at the moment, but ah could give ye a wee
grin if ye like.'

Overheard in butcher's in Glasgow.
'How much are they ribs?'
'Four pounds eighty a kilo.'
'Whit! Listen, ah widnae pay
that price fur ribs even if they
were attached tae Sean
Connery!'

Overheard at entrance to Buchanan
Galleries shopping complex. Mother
to two small boys.
'Listen, if yer gonnae make a racket fur heaven's sake dae
it quietly!'

Overheard on pavement outside toy shop in Edinburgh. Obviously a much-married couple.

'Quick! You need tae sort this lot oot, Sandy. Your weans an' ma weans are knockin' hell oot o' oor weans.'

Overheard at Glasgow Barras. Stall vendor selling electronic equipment.

'Attention youse lot! And here we have a thirty-two-inch plasma telly. Perfect fur watchin' Bargain Hunt and this is your bargain o' the day. Perfect apart frae the volume control which is stuck oan high. Forty-five quid tae the first hand that goes up. Aw come oan! Surely youse lot cannae turn this telly doon?'

In a lift in a Glasgow department store. Small man walks in, soaked to the skin.

'Looks like it's quite wet outside?'

'Listen, pal, afore ah came oot this morning ah wis over six fit.'

Overheard in Buchanan Galleries, Glasgow.

'He is a great one for the hand-wringing. If you see him at it he's probably going tae come oot wi' another lie.'

Overheard in Borders book shop, Glasgow.

'I was told by my father never to judge a sausage by its skin. But the cover on that book there, for example, bears no relation to its contents. Looks like somebody had a fit while holding a quill pen.'

'I actually very seldom look at fiction books. I'm into autobiographies and biographies this weather.'
'I should try to do that, too. The trouble with fiction is it is made up.'

Overheard in Greggs the bakers, Glasgow.
'Gonnae gie us a sausage roll, an' could ye take the meat oot? The wean's a vegetarian.'

Overheard in Gyle Shopping Centre, Edinburgh.
'Have you got yourself a dentist yet?'
'No, ah cannae get anybody to take me on.'
'My grandfather said he once removed a bad tooth with a piece of string tied round a doorknob, but I can't really believe that.'
'It would be a right laugh if the door opened the other way round!'

Overheard at Glasgow Barras. Stall selling watches.
'This watch has a jewel movement, is guaranteed for ten years, and I am not asking for a hundred pounds for it, not fifty pounds, not twenty pounds, not ten pounds, not even five pounds. One price only … a pound!'
'Aye, but does it go?'
'Sir! You put this watch on your wrist and anywhere you go, it goes!'

Overheard in Silverburn Shopping Centre.

'He spends most of his time in his garden shed. His wife told ma wife that immediately after his tea every night he is away out to the shed. Locks the door, tae. Sounds a bit suspicious to me, eh?'

'Have you seen his wife? Anybody would lock themselves in their shed if they had to sit and look at her dial aw night.'

Overheard in Art Deco furnishings shop, Edinburgh.

'Just look over there, Florence. Is that a gazunder filled with tea?'

'Oh. I thought you said pee!'

Overheard in Eye to Eye Opticians, Glasgow.

'It's just that I keep talking to myself, in fact I keep asking myself questions. It's amazing the smart answers I get back.'

Overheard in Vodafone shop, Edinburgh.
'Have you seen ma neighbour's new wean?'
'Aye, nice wee soul, but looks a bit haun' knitted tae me.'

Overheard in Morrisons supermarket, Ardrossan.
'She and her partner met on a blind date. She didnae like the look o' him at first and by the sound of it she's still no' all that keen. At least she's finally got hersel' a man.'

Overheard in Debenhams, Glasgow.
'Two thousand and nine was supposed to be the Year of Homecoming in Scotland. Well, ah wid just like oor Andrew tae come home wance afore midnight.'

Overheard in Next, Glasgow.
'I always say that a woman is at her best a wee bit later on in life. Probably forty is a nice age.'
'It is, especially if she's forty-five!'

Overheard in Asda, Paisley. Man and woman talking.
'They don't fight and argue for hours like we do. Just a couple o' words and it's over.'
'Aye, nae stamina, that pair.'

Overheard in chemist in Edinburgh.
'They do say the worse that medicine tastes the better it is for you.'

'Och, aw ye need tae take wi' it is a wee swally o' Lucozade an' whisky an' yer brand new.'

Overheard in Asda, Linwood.
'Ah don't like the tone o' that look ye just gave me.'
'Very funny, ha, ha.'

Overheard in butcher's in Hamilton.
'I know that I am getting wrinkles myself but she clearly doesn't use a moisturiser. It's getting to the time with her that the next stage will be grout!'

Overheard in butcher's in Kilmarnock, which has a sign outside, 'Noted Sausage Maker'.
'Can I ask, why have you a sign outside your shop saying, "Noted Sausage Maker"?'
'Well, ye see, madam, if they wurnae noted the meat would come oot the end.'

Overheard in Asda, Paisley.
'Well, what she tells everybody her age is is her own business.

But let me tell you this, she has been in her business for at least forty years.'

Overheard outside Primark, Greenock.
'No, I wear those Spanx knickers aw the time. They grip you like Ally McCoist would. Ah should be so lucky, eh?'

Overheard at the Barras, Glasgow.
'Ah think he plays whit they call "mind games" wi' me. Tries tae get me upset. He's really a bit o' a pain. An' the pain isnae in his mind, it's a bit lower doon than that.'

Overheard in Boots, Ayr.
'You're the talk o' the wash house, you know, you an' that man o' yours.'
'Ah don't care what everybody thinks. Just as long as ma mother doesnae find out.'

Overheard in butcher's in Paisley.
'Last year we were lucky an' got the last turkey they had in here. And it went cheap.'
'First time I've ever heard of a dead turkey going cheep.'

Overheard in shop in Leith.
'She's a wee cracker so she is. She looks exactly like her big sister but with a different shape of face, eyes and nose.'

Overheard in ladies' dress shop, Glasgow.

'Could I try on that black dress in the window, please?'

'There is only one answer to that. No, you must use the changing rooms.'

Overheard in John Lewis, Glasgow.

'See aw they extra-marital affairs they TV people keep having, how is it they get aw the action an' here's me at thirty-three still waitin' oan ma bus tae ecstasy?'

Overheard in pet shop in Glasgow.

'I want a goldfish for my son.'

'No problem. Would you like a wee aquarium?'

'Don't tell me ye keep them by their birth signs?'

Overheard in Topman, Edinburgh.

'Do you take English money up here?'

'Aye, as long as you'll take Scottish notes doon there.'

Overheard in Tesco, Glasgow.

'She told me the other day that she had spent three hours in the beauticians.'

'Probably only in for an estimate.'

Overheard in Asda, Paisley.

'A funny pair they are. They are noo an item. Ye can tell she's smitten by the way she looks at him, though she does look a wee bit squinty-eyed tae me. And as fur him, ma friend Elsie says that she has known him for years but still doesnae know him, if ye know whit ah mean.'

Overheard in newsagent's in Aberdeen.

'We spend twa pounds on the Saturday draw. Ah always go fur the lucky dip option. It gives you a wee surprise every Saturday night when ye check your numbers.'

'Have you ever won anything?'

'Naw.'

Overheard in Post Office in Kilmarnock.

'So how is it going with your new neighbours, then?'

'He's very nice but she has been in three times sponging aff me. In fact she wis in yesterday asking if ah had ony flour. Ah had tae smile, though; she wanted tae make a sponge cake.'

Overheard in newsagent's in Clydebank.

'How long were you in John Brown's Shipyard, Arthur?'

'About five feet seven.'

Overheard in large shop in Edinburgh.

'Wis that a good day ye had, Santa? Did ye keep aw the weans happy?'

'Ur ye kiddin'! This morning a wee lass wet ma trousers and ah had tae go hame and change at lunchtime.'

Overheard in butcher's in Falkirk.
'I think that turkey is o'er big for my oven.'
'Well that's your goose cooked, missus.'

Overheard in Morrisons, Edinburgh.
'Her room is always higgledy-piggledy. A right pig-sty. You would think they would learn you at the school tae keep things tidy.'

Overheard in hairdresser's in Edinburgh.
'We went to one of those murder weekends. It was super fun. They stage a couple of murders and you have to decide who the murderer is. Some of the guests were actors. My Frank's shirt got covered in the stuff they use as blood. I've given it a good scrub but it's murder to get out.'

Overheard in House of Fraser, Glasgow.
'Ah told ye last night ah loved ye. Have ah goat tae tell ye every two minutes, ya daft bitch?'

Overheard in Buchanan Galleries.
'And she is always so sarcastic. Makes that Anne Robinson look like an angel.'

Overheard in shop in Cumbernauld Shopping Centre.
'Ah would bring back the belt. Didnae dae me ony harm. In ma day they didnae need aw this nonsense o' security guys an' polis in the schools. When Big Daddy Marshall gave ye six o' the best ye didnae dae it again. Ever!'

Overheard in Slater's Menswear, Glasgow.
'But I do love you. That's why I want to look my best. It's for you.'
'Huh! See you, you remind me o' that Gazza, in fact you look a wee bit like him. Aw elbows an' mooth, and expecting tae score aw the time.'

Overheard in perfumery in Glasgow.
'Here's something I'm going to get you, Duncan. It says, "Help a man recharge his energy and renew his passions with this invigorating fragrance." '
'You'd better get me six bottles, pet.'

Overheard in hairdresser's in Paisley.
'Do you not think that people should be left to die in dignity? All this keeping them alive with tubes in them. Just let me pass on to the next world.'
'Is there another world?'
'Got to be. I reckon they transfer you to this other world, otherwise this one would get far too crowded.'
'A bit too deep for me, that.'

Overheard in garage at Phoenix Centre, Paisley.
'I've asked my manager, and he says we could stretch to fifteen hundred as your trade-in price.'
'I assume that's for a colour photo o' the car!'

Overheard in shoe shop in Edinburgh.
'The first half o' ma life was ruined by ma parents, the second half by my kids, and it's noo ma feet that's killin' me.'

Overheard in B&Q, Paisley.
'Furniture made wi' good wood doesnae come cheap. Doesnae grow on trees, you know!'

Overheard in newsagent's in Edinburgh.
'The problem is that I cannae find ma glasses without ma glasses!'

Overheard in Starbucks, Glasgow.
'I overdid it on Saturday night. We were at this party and they kept on filling up my glass. See on Sunday morning, I had a mouth like a chemical toilet. Think ah'll have a gargle o' Domestos.'

Overheard in hairdresser's in Helensburgh.
'They're not going to tell Auntie Winnie that they're emigrating to Queensland. They say they'll send her an email once they get there, and I know for a fact she doesn't have a computer.'

Overheard at Boots Counter in Glasgow Airport. Young woman explaining to assistant.
'See when ah fancy a guy ah need tae go tae the toilet. An' if ah really, really fancy him ah get diarrhoea. He's on oor flight tae Majorca. Wis standing behind us in the queue. Ah wonder if he's goin' tae oor resort?'

Overheard in Boots, Ayr.
'I get so fed up with all those junk emails. "Pass on to another twelve people or something will happen to you." I just give it the old "delete" button, and the only bad thing that happens to me is that, as sure as God makes little apples, I get another pile of junk emails in.'

Overheard at supermarket check-out in Edinburgh.
'It came as quite a shock to the family. They are quite a quiet lot. Keep themselves to themselves. They apparently didn't know she was pregnant. In fact her mother was putting her on a diet. Just shows you, doesn't it. Then I heard she was quite promiscuous.'
'So, do we know who the father is?'
'Heaven knows. It's like that Pick 'n' Mix you used to get in Woolies.'

Overheard at hairdresser's in Newtongrange.
'Ah'll just cut a wee bit off the front here. Make it look modern so it will.'
'That'll be the first fringe benefit I've had in fifty years, dearie.'

Overheard in Silverburn Shopping Centre.
'At least before credit cards you always knew how much ye were skint.'

Overheard outside estate agent's in Glasgow.
'Just look at this advert. "A rare opportunity to acquire this substantial tenement property." Ah know a wummin who lives up that close and to call her clatty would be a compliment.'

Overheard in chemist in Paisley.
'He's wan o' they folks that have went from hero tae zero. Big job in a bank he had. Noo, look at him. Lucky if he could get a job in Tesco fillin' shelves.'
'I wouldn't exactly say that filling the shelves in Tesco is zero. My nephew does that and apparently quite enjoys it!'
'Oh. Right.'

Overheard in hairdresser's in Glasgow.
'She was double-timing him for years and years. He always had to play second fiddle. And now the joke is that the polis have been up at his hoose. Apparently he has been fiddling at his work, tae.'

Overheard in Jenners, Loch Lomond Shores.
'I think you are much older than you look.'
'I don't know how to take that!'

Overheard in Oak Mall, Greenock.
'How did the bus tour up north go?'
'Wonderful. What a bargain. Real value for money. The hotels were comfortable and the food quite good. The only moan I had was when we stopped at public toilets for a comfort break on the way back. They were boggin'! The smell would have choked you. Ah just told the driver they were crap!'

Overheard in Next, Glasgow.
'My Peter's so good tae me. And so's our Susan. I've got to say children are a great comfort to you in your old age.'
'Aye, and if they're anything like mine they help you reach it faster.'

Overheard in Marks and Spencer, Argyle Street, Glasgow.
'See if I have cheese on toast before I go to bed, I get great dreams. I cannae remember what they are but sometimes it's like going to the movies.'

Overheard in Marks and Spencer, Silverburn.
'You can tell somebody's age by the way their hands look. I read this in a magazine at the dentist. Ah've been putting hand cream on them ever since. Ma man says ah'm a bit slippery tae get hold of in bed, the dirty devil!'

Overheard in hairdresser's in East Kilbride.
'I'm no' speaking tae her at the moment.'
'Should you not try an' bury the hatchet?'
'Aye, in her heid!'

Overheard in John Lewis's jewellery department, Glasgow.
'Look at they dangly earrings, Eleanor. Ah love that wan wi' the hoops and the wee bell thing at the bottom. Whit dae ye think wid go wi' that?'
'How about a budgie?'

Overheard in Marks and Spencer cafeteria, Ayr.
'It's a good half-hour's walk from here.'
'Let me tell you, there's nothing good about walking for half an hour at ma age.'

Overheard in hairdresser's in Largs.

'Listen dearie, when you get to ma age it's not The X Factor you watch. It's something more appropriate like One Foot in the Grave.'

Overheard in Cameron Toll shopping centre, Edinburgh.

'It makes me flaming mad. He just turns over and he's away. I can tell by his breathing. Never really snores, just a wee snort noo and again. And there's me lying there for hours trying tae go tae sleep, ma legs going like jitterbugs.'

Overheard in Glasgow club.

'Ma old boyfriend had a clapped-out jalopy. An' he wis as bad as his car. When you were up for it he refused to start. His battery was flat, he used to say, and it usually wis.'

Overheard in hairdresser's in Edinburgh.

'You have got a fine head of hair, sir.'

'Don't be daft, I'm nearly bald.'

'I meant you have a fine head of hair for me to cut.'

'Aye, but do you cut yer price?'

Overheard in chemist in Aberdeen.
'See this business of "man-flu"; all men get it when they have a cold.'
'Tell me about it. Every time mine gets a cold he thinks it's terminal.'

Overheard in hairdresser's in Edinburgh.
'Imagine! He fainted at the passing-out parade. You've got to have a secret wee laugh, sure you do?'

Overheard in service station, 'Ye Can Gang Faur and Fare Waur', near Aberdeen.
'I just had tea and toast this morn. I'm trying to discipline myself. See if I can get under the twelve stones.'
'But you've just had a plate of macaroni and chips.'
'I know, but I usually have more than that at lunch.'
'To be honest I think you're kidding yourself. Remember last night we had curry and chips.'
'But I didn't eat all of my chips.'
'No, but you certainly ate most of mine.'

Overheard in Cardwell Garden Centre, Gourock.
'I always plant my early spring bulbs mid-September to the end of October. The earth is still warm and moist and the roots grow right away.'
'How do you know the roots grow right away if you cannae see them?'
'Dae you always ask awkward questions, son?'

Overheard in hairdresser's in Glasgow.
'She's goat very limited intelligence, tae pit it mildly. I think her mother must have got her brain oot an Argos catalogue.'

Overheard inside Marks and Spencer, Stirling. Woman giving her man a dig with her shopping bag and having a moan.
'You never communicate with me. If ah didnae have other women tae talk to ah'd never hear a word. Dae ye hear me, ya big numptie?'

Overheard in Next, Glasgow.
'He's wan o' they Fire and Flood restoration experts. Mind you, who ever heard of a fire in the middle o' a flood, ah ask ye?'

Overheard in chemist in Glasgow.
'Do you have something that will prevent my dandruff repeatedly coming back?'
'How about an axe? Just kidding, madam.'

Overheard in chemist in Airdrie.
'I find if I am all stressed and tense then I tend to look older. You've got to look after your emotional health with muscle relaxation exercises. Forget Botox. Wash your face three times a day in hot, soapy water.'
'Ah know some folks who obviously don't even wash their face three times a year.'

Overheard in Lidl, Glasgow.
'She got a new knee three weeks ago. I was talking to her yesterday. Amazing what they can do nowadays. Mind you they still cannae cure the cold. I've had this cold now for months. I think I'll just go and get myself a new nose.'

Overheard in shop in Renfrew.
'He is really a bit of a rebel without a cause.'
'Well, our Michael is a bit of a mystery as well. If anything he is a rebel without a clue, so he is.'

Overheard in hairdresser's in Edinburgh.
'He was caught by the police and was charged with driving under the influence. Told them he had drunk a very generous glass of port at a dinner. Didn't tell them about the half bottle of brandy he had, too.'

Overheard in Glasgow shop.
'He was getting quite bald anyway, even though he is in his late twenties. So he just got the lot off. Once you get used to it it looks okay. Actually makes him younger rather than older. That's the bald truth of it, if you'll excuse the expression.'

Overheard at wives' birthday section in card shop in Glasgow.
'Are you managing to find something suitable for your wife, sir?'
'Listen, dear. Did you ever see that film Mission Impossible?'

Overheard in Pollokshields.
'She is apparently going with this chap who is seventy. She's just forty.'
'So, has he plenty of money?'
'Her mother says he has three pensions. She also said, and you have to laugh, that if they do get married they will need to live near a school. I take it she's at the kidding.'
'And at seventy he's a bit old to be at the kidding tae, eh?'

Overheard in a chemist in Falkirk.
'Where are your laxatives, please?'
'Laxatives?'
'Listen, when ye get tae ma age you'll know aw aboot laxatives.'

Overheard in Marks and Spencer, Argyle Street, Glasgow.
'See her over there standing at the check-out? Ah remember her

fae way back. She wis always ugly, tae pit it mildly. Somebuddy told me wance that two weeks efter she wis born her mother tried tae have an abortion.'

Overheard in clothes shop in Edinburgh.
'Me? I would like a pair of jeans that will zip all the way up without me jumping up and down and my partner holding them.'
'Sounds a bit naughty.'
'Well, you never know your luck.'

Overheard in Princes Mall Shopping Centre, Edinburgh.
'I'm up about five times a night. It's an enlarged prostate. Same during the day. Need to urinate frequently. Now I only go into a department store with a loo.'

Overheard in greengrocer's in Glasgow.
'Hey! You're jumping the queue. We've been here for five minutes.'
'Sorry. Ah didnae know this was the wrong end of the queue. Ah just want some totties.'
'Well totties have eyes and so have you!'

Overheard in Silverburn Shopping Centre.
'Hello, there. Nice to see you both. The last time we met, you were just about to go for a jaunt to London for shopping and the theatre.'

'Don't talk to me about these four days. The price of a cup of coffee in the hotel was ridiculous. You would have needed a mortgage. We spent a fortune. My credit card melted and my wallet's still gasping for air.'

Overheard in chemist in Edinburgh.
'We went on a run in the car to Peebles at the weekend. Could hardly get out of the car for the wind and the cold. Freezing it was. I must say I've got my doubts about this business of global warming. Tom says he is going to have a farmer friend of his have his cows fart more. Apparently that helps to warm the world up. Crazy, isn't it.'

Overheard in Tesco, Port Glasgow.
'This is the second lot of scans he has had. Apparently they

misplaced the first ones. The National Health Service was supposed to be improving. They have timetables for everything now, and yet seeing the doctor is no good without the scan results. And these new pills he is on don't seem to agree with him either.'

'Poor man. What about his legs?'

'They're a bit better, thank you. I don't think there is anywhere in his body that's right. He's been like that all his life. No doctor in this country will ever be made redundant while Jack's still alive.'

Overheard in shop in Paisley.
'When I go and stay with my daughter, the neighbour comes in and feeds my cats. It's very good of her because she is allergic to them. Makes her eyes go red. Actually she's blind.'

Overheard in Harvey Nichols, Edinburgh.
'The trouble is, you see, Margaret, it's my bottom. It's quite big unfortunately and I'm so conscious of it when I wear trousers, even in front of Eddie at home.'

'I thought you always wore the trousers in your house!'

Overheard outside furniture shop in Glasgow.
'Look at that leather suite. No deposit and twelve easy payments efter six months.'

'That suite would be ruined efter six months with ma weans all over it. And let me tell you, there is no such thing as an easy payment.'

Overheard in Edinburgh shop.
'We did a tour last year to Balmoral and the Highlands. We also did some monster spotting at Loch Ness. Saw nothing. The only monster was a huge woman on the bus who told outrageous tales and really got up my hump.'

Overheard in Jenners, Edinburgh.
'She always had great hopes for him. Did he finally manage to graduate? Ah know he had a few re-sits.'
'Him! He's thick. Would be as useless as a lifeguard in a car wash.'

Overheard in Argyll Arcade, Glasgow.
'Hey, just look at ye. Ye look a million dollars wi' that tan. Where did ye get it?'
'Crete. The weather was fab. Only got back last night.'
'So where are you working nowadays?'
'Ah'm no'. Ah'm aff on the sick.'

Overheard in Marks and Spencer, Braehead. Little boy who looked about four.
'Hey, mammy, which wan dae ye want an' ah'll stick it up ma jouks.'

Overheard in ladies' dress shop in
Silverburn Shopping Centre.
'Do you think my bum looks
big in this?'
'Naw, but yer big belly does.'

Overheard in barber's in
Edinburgh.
'I wasn't really too struck with
her.'
'But you went out with her at
least three times.'
'Three times too many, believe
me.'
'So why did you go out with her?'
'She wis mostly paying.'

Overheard in shop in Braehead Shopping Centre.
'Sorry, ah wis talking tae masel' there. Ah even laugh at ma ain
jokes. An' half o' them are rotten, tae. Pathetic, ain't it?'

Overheard in card shop in Glasgow.
'Did ye get ony Valentine cards this year, Betty?'
'Aye, ah goat wan. It wis lousy. Probably frae "that wan".'
'Who is "that wan"?'
'Him! Ma man, the dope himsel'.'

Overheard in Morrisons, Edinburgh. Customer to lady filling shelves.
'Dae ye stock ony o' they boxes o' Ferocious chocolates?'
'Ferocious chocolates?'
'Aye, ye ken, they're advertised oan the telly. Wee balls wrapped in gold wi' chocolate, an' nuts inside them.'

Overheard in butcher's in Dundee.
'Gie's a bone, hen, wi' some meat oan it, wid ye?'
'Here's wan. That'll be wan pound fifty.'
'Listen! It's fur the dug, no tae pit oan ma mantlepiece.'

Overheard in health food shop in Edinburgh.
'Sorry for the delay in helping you but I'm on my own today. The other assistant is off ill.'

Overheard in Tesco in Edinburgh.
'We're going down to the Borders this weekend. Probably stay at a B&B. Ah hope the weather's good. Have you been away lately?'
'We took a cheepie airline to Paris last month. The hotel was fine but the weather was awful. Coming down in stair rods. We went to the Louvre to see the Mona Lisa. I had to laugh – there was a wee man from Glasgow beside us who said that her face was no oil painting.'

OVERHEARD IN RESTAURANTS AND CAFES

Overheard in restaurant in Leith.
'See these so called anti-ageing creams. I don't think they really work. Don't laugh, but I read in a magazine that the best cream to put on your face, not near your eyes mind you, is cream for haemorrhoids. No kidding.'
'Do you put piles of it on, then?!'

Overheard in restaurant in Edinburgh.
'I think he's a bit inadequate. A bit of an oddball, really.'
'Well I wish I was an oddball. He drives a new Merc.'

Overheard in café in Stirling.
'She says that it was only when a man approached her that she realised she had wandered into the red light district.'
'And you believed her? Probably just trying to pay for her holiday.'

Overheard in restaurant in Edinburgh.
'My husband's uncle played the concertina, you know, a squeezebox. Had strong arms. Not unsurprisingly he was a great hugger, too.'

Overheard in café in Dundee.

'Naw, naw, her teeth are big choppers, definitely false. We wis wance oan a bus tour thegither an' ah could hear her wallies rattlin' every time the coach hit a bump.'

Overheard in McDonald's in Greenock.

'Naw, she's an' auld maid, so she is. Wid die wi' her legs up if a man propositioned her.'

'Well, she wid need tae pit her legs up, sure she wid!'

Overheard in pensioners' lunch club in Glasgow.

'I love to get down on the floor to play with the grandchildren. Then comes the big challenge – getting up again.'

Overheard in fish and chip shop in Airdrie.

'Gonnae no' dae that, son.'

'Gonnae no' dae whit?'

'Gonnae stop flickin' the salt all o'er the place. Looks like snow.'

'But ah like salt wi' ma chips.'

'Looks tae me as though ye like chips wi' yer salt!'

Overheard in café at the Beatson Oncology Centre, Glasgow.
'She might be thirteen but ah bet she knows mair aboot sex than ah dae. Telling her anything aboot the facts o' life wid be like giving oor wee goldfish a bath.'

Overheard in café in Gartnavel Hospital.
'Two cappuccinos and a raisin cookie, please.'
'Don't talk tae me aboot raisin cookies. Ah've got a right cookie at hame, and see raisin' him oot his bed in the morn, it's murder.'

Overheard in restaurant in Glasgow.
'We were in Mull last year. Weather was mixed but the boys enjoyed it. I was thinking of going again this year. I'm mulling it over at the moment.'

Overheard in chip shop in Glasgow.
'Ah'm away hame noo. Ah don't know whether tae wash ma herr the night, watch EastEnders, or just go tae bed wi the Dandy.'

Overheard in deli in Edinburgh between a customer and helpful Polish assistant.
'Does your soup of the day have any wheat in it? Ah'm allergic to wheat.'
'No.'
'Good. Then ah'll have a plate of your soup.'
'Would you like roll with it?'

Overheard in restaurant in Edinburgh.
'We got the "sing-along" version of the Mamma Mia! DVD. We've had it on umpteen times. The neighbours will think the wife has changed into a Dancing Queen.'

Overheard in café on board Arran ferry.
'And unfortunately I have this small birthmark on my neck.'
'Oh, yes, I see it. How long have you had it?'

Overheard outside restaurant in Glasgow.
'I've eaten too much. Full up I am and full o' wind. I was glad to get oot o' there an' have a right good fart.'

Overheard in café in Glasgow.
'Surely there are only so many ways to have sex. You know we only have a limited number of orifices. He keeps thinking up new ideas. It's quite exciting sometimes.'

Overheard in McDonald's in Stirling.
'I know why Peggy took the huff. She'd on a new dress and you didn't mention it.'

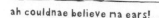

'Och, she's always buying new clothes. What was so special about that one?'

'Surely you couldnae miss the cleavage she was displaying?'

'I certainly did notice. Reminded me o' the Pass o' Glencoe, so it did.'

Overheard in restaurant in Glasgow.

'See this Battle o' the Bulge we are all fighting. Well, ah wid need sodgers standin' outside bakers' shops tae help me win it.'

Overheard outside café in Glasgow

'Hello. Are you William Craig?'

'Yes. Do I know you?'

'You should. You sat behind me in Shawlands Primary school.'

'Sorry, I didn't recognise you.'

'James Smyth.'

'Oh, James, now I remember you. You were good at the football. But how did you recognise me?'

'I remembered your cough. You spluttered down ma neck for years.'

Overheard in café in North Berwick.

'Naw, naw. He could eat for Scotland. Never seems to stop. I don't think there is anything he doesn't like. And there isn't a pick on him. Ah wish I was like that. It's so unfair. I've only got to squint sideways at a bar o' chocolate and I put on pounds.'

Overheard in Burger King in Glasgow.
'You wouldn't believe it. She's as skinny as a rake and she puts in two full teaspoonfuls of sugar in her coffee. Says it keeps her sweet. It would give me sweet damn all but a pile o' fat.'

Overheard in Marks and Spencer's café at Braehead.
'Do you want more coffee?'
'Aye, sure ah refuse nothing but blows, as ma auld granny used tae say when she wis sober.'

Overheard in pensioners' lunch club in Glasgow.
'They were in this really posh hotel in London. She went to the loo in the middle of the night and there was a live rat in the bowl. She calmly put down the lid and phoned reception. They sent up a porter who put on rubber gloves and removed it. Seems they have had this sort of thing before. They got a free meal in the hotel on the strength of it. But imagine, you sit down and a rat bites your bum.'

Overheard in burger bar in Glasgow.
'Ah wis thinking o' talkin' ma husband intae getting' wan o' them bidets. They're supposed to be very hygienic. But oor Billy wid probably just pee in it.'

Overheard in restaurant in Edinburgh. Customer talking to manager.
'How far away is your kitchen?'

'It is downstairs, sir.'
'We have been waiting now for almost half-an-hour. Have you not got a dumb waiter?'
'No, sir.'
'Well we've certainly got a dumb waiter at our table.'

Overheard in café in Argyle Street, Glasgow.
'We put an offer in for the house, then our lawyer discovered a problem with the title deeds. Something about a public right of way. So needless to say, that was that. Now we are looking for a bungalow in the Mearns that doesn't have a public walkway running through the lounge.'

Overheard in restaurant in Glasgow.
'You do know her. She's quite tall and lanky.'
'Oh, her. Aye, ah do know her. But you obviously haven't been too close to her.'
'How's that.'
'I would say she's more like tall and manky.'

Overheard in pensioners' lunch club in Glasgow.
'The only romantic lane ah now go down is Memory Lane. Me and Stuart used tae love a wee cuddle when we were courting aw these years ago. Nice tae have memories like that. Mind you wi' aw the crime nooadays I'd be frightened even tae go doon Memory Lane in the daylight.'

Overheard in café in Edinburgh.
'Every time I pick up a packet of something in the supermarket it seems to say, "May contain traces of nuts." It makes me laugh when I think of my hubby doing his family tree last year. He certainly found plenty traces of nuts.'

Overheard in café in Gourock.
'Fur seems to be back in, you know. It's acceptable. Very few people seem to protest this weather. I mentioned it to my husband that I fancied one and he said he would get me a donkey jacket.'

Overheard in café in Glasgow.
'Ah don't know whether it wis the drink or the wacky-baccy ah took at the Bells, but anyway ah ended up doolally.'

Overheard in café in Renfrew.
'We like that Antiques Roadshow that's on on a Sunday night. We have been watching it for years.'

'I like that programme, too. But the only thing we have is some early MFI furniture with screws missing.'

Overheard in café in Glasgow.
'Apparently you can relieve flatulence and diarrhoea by adding a pinch of grated nutmeg to your food. It slows down the movement of food through the gastro-intestinal tract.'
'I think I'll need to try that with Bill. Every time he gets up off a chair he farts.'

Overheard in café in Leith.
'Gave her the heave, so he did. An' she told me she was a virgin when they first met.'
'Well, she must have met him in primary one. In secondary school they were queuing up.'

Overheard in café in the Gallowgate, Glasgow.
'Isn't it amazing that salmon find their way home from the ocean to spawn in exactly the same location they were born.'
'Well, according to ma father I was spawned at the back of the bus garage in London Road. They've pulled it down now, so that's me had it.'

Overheard in café in Glasgow.

'The pair of them went to Taiwan for their honeymoon. Ma mither says she's chased plenty of men in her time, and noo she's finally tai-ed wan up.'

Overheard in restaurant in Brodick.

'If I want something done I just forbid my fourteen-year-old to do it, and nine times out of ten, quick as a flash, it's done.'

Overheard in tearoom in Edinburgh.

'My husband and his mates won the big quiz at the club last night. I've got to say his general knowledge is very good.'
'Yes, he seems to know everything.'
'Good Lord, ah hope not.'

Overheard in café in Glasgow.

'He got a standing ovation at the end though ah didnae stand masel'. You know, wi ma slipped disc an' that. Anyways, ah didnae like his brand o' humour. In fact, ah didnae understand half his jokes. Oor dug's funnier.'

Overheard in café in Newtongrange.
'Don't talk to me about stubborn males. I've had three in my time, and ye couldnae change any o' them, unless when they were wearing nappies.'

Overheard in tearoom in Edinburgh.
'I actually quite like men who are, I don't know how to put it, a wee bit fruity. Like that Colin in the office.'
'Him! I was talking to him before lunch and I wouldn't say he's fruity; more like a vegetable.'

Overheard in restaurant in Edinburgh.
'He just won't admit to himself that he is getting older.'
'I've got one like that at home, too. Thinks he's a Timelord. Doctor Who I call him.'

Overheard in café in Glasgow.
'That one is forever opening her big mouth and showing herself up. She'd be dangerous if she had a personality.'

Overheard in restaurant in Edinburgh.
'Every morning we are into the same routine. Out come his pills and out come mine. We sit there like a pair o' junkies throwing back the drugs. Then, usually about an hour later or so, he asks me if he has taken his medication. The silly old goat.'

Overheard in restaurant in Glasgow.

'I'm getting quite deaf. I am actually thinking of going for a hearing aid. The only thing that puts me off is old Morag next door. Hers whistles away like a kettle.'

Overheard in café in Bridge of Weir.

'I can remember when the track was a railway and the train from Kilmacolm came steaming up the line. Nice to have memories like that.'

'And I can remember my father walking up beside the line on a Saturday, and he was usually steamin', too.'

Overheard in café in Paisley.

'I just love my cats. I was brought up in a household with cats. My next door neighbour clearly doesn't like them. Always making catty comments, she is.'

Overheard in café in Perth.

'She's just eighteen and at the weekends she becomes a night owl. Then about four in the morning in comes ma wee homing pigeon.'

Overheard in café in Glasgow.

'I know they say that variety is the spice of life, and she's had plenty of spice, believe me. The only time she draws a line it's with an eyebrow pencil.'

Overheard in café in Edinburgh.
'She keeps interrupting the conversation and then gets offended when someone else tries to talk. I'm actually quite sure she invents things just so she can keep talking. I had an aunt who was just the same. Ended up in a care home and drove everybody mad.'

Overheard in Burger King in Glasgow.
'Listen, dad, ah'm old enough tae stand on my own two feet.'
'And if ye stand on mine ye'll get a skelp. Ma corns are killing me.'

Overheard in sandwich bar in Glasgow.
'She pokes her nose into everything. You can hardly get on with your work for that yin interfering. And fussy! Everything has got to be perfect. Got a breath on her like a step-mother's deid dug. She's intae the hard stuff at night. I shouldn't really have told you that. I'm telling it to you in confidence because it was actually told tae me in confidence.'

Overheard in tearoom in Edinburgh.
'I heard she is unbelievably modest. Her husband told my husband she needs to draw the curtains to change her mind. And her with four children, too.'

Overheard in café in North Berwick.
'Have you ever seen such wee, skinny thighs? They remind me o'
a wish-bone at Christmas.'

Overheard in café in Glasgow.
'An absolute pain in the butt, so she is. An' her herr looks like a
hoor's knickers turned ootside in an' tied wi' pink ribbon. It's a
pity her mother hadnae practised birth control.'

Overheard in café in Glasgow.
'He's got a company who specialise in family trees to dig back
and get all the details. Now he won't tell anybody what they
found. Bit suspicious if you ask me.'

Overheard in Burger King, Glasgow.
'Her back is noo full o' tattoos. See when we were in Corfu, every
time she walked along the beach it wis like going tae the pictures.'

Overheard in café in Glasgow.
'No man is going to make a fool out of me!'
'Who did, then?'
'You're getting a bit cheeky!'

Overheard in café in Paisley.
'He can get you fake CDs and DVDs dead cheap. Fakes are the
new "must-have" item, noo.'

Overheard in BHS cafeteria, Glasgow.

'Could I have another portion of butter for my roll, please?'

'That'll be another fifteen pence. But don't blame me, it's "they other wans" that make up the rules.'

'Well just tell "they other wans" I'm not having another butter. The rolls are too big fur just one portion of butter.'

'Right, I'll tell them tae make wee rolls next time.'

Overheard in restaurant in Edinburgh.

'Actually I'm not so good at mixing at parties. I usually only talk to strangers if I know them quite well.'

Overheard in Burger King in Glasgow.

'The trouble wi' me is ah open ma mooth an' ma brain goes fur a joy-ride.'

Overheard in McDonald's in Maryhill. Mother to daughter, who looks about five.

'Naw, ye're no' getting ony mair chips. Ye'll get o'er fat an' no' get a man.'

Overheard in restaurant in Clydebank.

'He is amazing for ninety. Votes every week on Big Brother, he's got an iPod and listens to Take That, texts all his friends, hasn't got a hair left on his head, and now he's doing a number with a widow in the same building.'

Overheard in café in Glasgow.
'Did ye go and get yer flu jag?'
'Aye, yesterday. Mind you last year ah got a wee touch o' flu a couple o' days after the jag. It didnae come tae much, thank goodness.'
'So it just flew, then!'

Overheard in café in Kilmarnock.
'Does your Bill still go out running every night in all weathers?'
'Not at the moment. He's strained his hamsters.'

Overheard in café in Hamilton.
'She is obsessed with anything to do with babies, and she's pushing fifty. The next thing will be she'll be pushing a pram.'

Overheard in Green Welly in Tyndrum.
'I think he secretly fancies you.'
'Don't be silly. Do you really think so?'
'I've never seen a more serious case of "love with the lid on" in my life.'

Overheard in tearoom in Glasgow.
'He's nothing but a hooligan. Will end up in jail. You mark ma words. Apparently battered somebuddy last month in that fish an' chip shop round the corner.'

Overheard in café in Hamilton.
'Him! Wee men in white coats will come an' take him away and shove tubes o' Smarties doon his throat.'
'How come?'
''Cause he's a right tube an' needs smarter brains.'

Overheard in café in Glasgow.
'It was freezing last night staunin' in the queue waiting tae get in tae the disco. Ah wis shivering.'
'Why didn't you wear a coat?'
'Don't be daft. I would look stupid. Naebuddy wears a coat nooadays.'

Overheard in café in Edinburgh.
'Hey, did you just pass gas?'
'Well ma father used to say, "May the wind at your back always be yer ain."'

Overheard in tearoom in Glasgow.
'Unfortunately we had to get rid o' our dog. Broke ma heart it did. But she was totally unsuitable fur a multi-storey. Never

could understand that she should only do her business outside. She was always choking tae get back up the stairs to pee in the hoose.'

Overheard in café in Edinburgh.
'Some o' them Christmas lights that people put up are just tacky, ah say. See all these Santas, reindeer and stuff? Junk, ah say. It's all right if you have kids but with it just being me and him ah'm not fussed, ah say. Ah just stick up the Christmas cards. Ah like to make it feel like Christmas, ah say.'

Overheard in café in Glasgow.
'You couldnae be up tae them nooadays. The burglars tried tae get intae that newsagent's shop at the corner and when they found they couldnae get in they stole the burglar alarm that wis outside. Imagine burglars stealin' a burglar alarm. Whit fur, ah ask ye?'

Overheard in queue at Burger King, Glasgow.
'That wan dresses right quaint, so she does. Looks like a picture on an auld biscuit tin ma granny used tae have.'

Overheard in café in Paisley.
'My ears have been burning all morning. They say that if they're not talking about you then you're not interesting.'
'Aye, well you are very interesting! No' many folks have had three husbands.'

Overheard in a
café in Stirling.
'See that
family? Well
ah'm gonnae
come back as a flying coo
an' do naughty things over the hale
lot o' them.'

Overheard in ladies' toilet in café in Edinburgh.
Mother talking to small girl.
'Are you going to do a wee tinkle or a wee plop, dear?'
'No, a huge, big jobbie, Mummy.'

Overheard in restaurant in Dundee.
'Actually I prefer Loch Lomond or Flower o' Scotland. Anything is
better than that dirge, God Save the Queen. Probably even bores
the pants aff the Royals.'

Overheard in tearoom in Edinburgh.
'The cruise was just lovely. We met some nice Americans on
board. They're always friendly and with such nice manners.
That's what we lack in this country, manners. They should teach
good manners in the schools. It's not sums they should teach,
it's manners that count.'

Overheard in restaurant in Glasgow.

'We used to be minimalists when it came to the house but we decided to change. We got some gold taps, cost a fortune mind you, and some fur-embellished upholstery. We also got some flamboyant colours for our fabrics, red and yellow. And you know lime green and aubergine are in now, too.'

'Aye, we need dark glasses tae sit in the front room, noo, sure we do, dear.'

'Don't listen tae him. Nae taste! Ma parents picked him out for me. Ah wid hate tae think I chose him masel'.'

'Don't listen tae her. Chased me all over Glasgow tae get me, she did.'

Overheard in tearoom in Edinburgh.

'I'll never go back to that café again. Every time you walk in the door you get hit by a fog of chip fat and armpits.'

Overheard in restaurant in Edinburgh. Customer to owner.

'Do you never get terribly harassed in here when it's busy?'

'The only harassment I ever get in here is when I give a dozen women one bill. Drive you batty so it would.'

Overheard in McDonald's in Glasgow.
'The first job they gave him in the factory he made a fist o' it. But he's knuckled down and noo he is doing a good job.'

Overheard in tearoom in Glasgow.
'My uncle lived until he was eighty-eight. He was a heavy smoker, always seemed to have a fag hanging from his lip. Some people get away wi' it and some don't. Mind you I don't think there is much pleasure in old age. Nothing but liver spots and arthritis.'

Overheard in Starbucks in Buchanan Street, Glasgow.
'The only thriving industries in this country are the Job Centres and prisons. It's the fault o' them comedians in that big gas showroom in Edinburgh.'
'Which gas showroom?'
'The Parliament!'

Overheard in restaurant in Glasgow.
'He's now a tree surgeon. You know, pruning, hedge-trimming, lopping branches. Funny word "surgeon". He probably mostly only runs about wi' an axe.'

Overheard in café in Glasgow.

'Paris was full of those "living statues". Ah don't know how they can stay still for so long. We saw one dressed as Charlie Chaplin on the Champs-Elysées. He was sitting in a box and he winked at everybody going by. I winked back. A bit of a comedian he was.'

Overheard in tearoom in Glasgow.

'See they electricians and plumbers that advertise in the paper, half o' them are cowboys. Then they never turn up. Probably away rustling.'

Overheard in café in Edinburgh.

'He is quite a businessman. Runs a couple of restaurants now.'
'I thought he had fish shops?'
'No, with the North Sea costs and quotas the business was floundering.'

Overheard in tearoom in Edinburgh.

'She fancies Barry Manilow. Ah don' see it masel'. No' wi' that conk. He's aw right if you keep yer eyes closed and just listen.'

Overheard in chip shop in Kirkcaldy.
'I always eat a balanced diet. A poke o' chips in each hand!'

Overheard in café in Motherwell.
'It's the feeling of nausea that gets me. Ah've got pills frae the doctor to stop it but I still cannae help but feel nauseous. It wid fair sicken ye.'

Overheard in fish and chip shop in Perth.
'Definitely not him wi' aw they plooks. Ah wouldnae go oot wi' him even if he farted gold bricks.'

Overheard in café in Renfrew
'His father was the manager in the shipyard. He wid have got naewhere in this world if his father hadnae have been born before him.'

Overheard in restaurant in Perth.
'And the price that they charge now for Christmas meals, it's ridiculous. You're not eating turkey, what you are eating is a whole pile of profit.'

Overheard in café in Braehead Shopping Centre.
'Unfortunately he has gone blind in one eye and the other is now not so good. Says it's really quite a blessing as he cannae see anything to worry aboot, noo.'

Overheard in a café in Dunoon.

'We went tae a farmers' market a couple o' weeks back. The organic vegetables have some odd shapes but at least you know they're no' full o' chemicals. Just coos' "you-know-what".'

Overheard in takeaway restaurant in Glasgow.

'Can ye no' hurry up? Ah'm starvin'. This must be the slowest fast-food shop in the country!'

Overheard in tearoom. Old couple having afternoon tea. The old gentleman giving advice to waitress.

'Listen, dear. The secret of good health is an aspirin a day, a glass of red wine every night, and no sex on Sundays.'

'Don't listen to him, dear. His wild oats are now only All-Bran and prunes.'

Overheard in café in Glasgow.

'She fairly fancies herself, but if you ask me she looks like Long John Silver wi' a spindle shank.'

Overheard in tearoom in Edinburgh.

'He has got a perfectly formed wee bum. I cannae take ma eyes off it. It gives me the inclinations.'

OVERHEARD ON TRANSPORT

Overheard on bus in Leith.

'You irritate me, Charles. And you always irritated my mother. No wonder she gave you funny looks.'

'Listen, Sylvia, the Prime Minister irritates you, half the programmes on the telly irritate ye, ma pals irritate ye. It's a wonder you don't have that irritable bowel syndrome!'

Overheard in Perth. Two ladies talking at bus stop.

'Tomorrow I've got to go to the dentist. A filling came out. I'm not looking forward to it. The last time I was there I was nearly an hour in the chair. Terrified I was.'

'Ah'm the same. Ah hate going tae the dentist. The only good thing aboot it is they don't weigh ye.'

Overheard by passenger in car. Two ladies were off to shop in Glasgow, but their car had been stopped by a police patrol car on the M8. The driver put down her window and switched off the engine. A policeman appeared and stuck his head in the window.

'Do you know what speed you were doing, madam?'

'Well, ah do know ah wis going a wee bit fast, officer.'

'We clocked you at eighty-two miles per hour, madam.'
'Sorry, but ah'm late for ma cancer treatment in the Beatson at Gartnavel Hospital.'
'Oh, I see. But can you prove this?'
'How does this grab you, officer?' she said as she whipped off her wig.
'Oh, right. Well, eh, sorry. I won't book you this time, but watch your speed in future.'
'Thank you, officer.'
'First time cancer ever did me ony good!' observed the driver.

Overheard on bus in Burnside.
'I've visited my dentist twice in the last week. She couldn't find out what was causing the pain. I was driven halfway up the wall. Then she finally located the abscess that was the root of the problem.'

Overheard on bus in Falkirk.
'Still very well mannered but awfa doddery he is. When he shakes your hand you can feel a wee tremble. Forty years ago when ah looked at him it wis ma knees that used to tremble.'

Overheard at bus stop near Oban.

'When's the next bus, dearie?'

'It won't arrive for an hour.'

'Och, it'll no' take me lang tae wait for an hour.'

Overheard outside Glasgow Central Station.

'Could somebuddy gie me a couple o' quid fur a wee meal? Ah'm starving.'

'A couple o' quid?'

'Awright then, wan quid. Deal or no deal?'

Overheard on bus in Edinburgh.

'He is a widower now.'

'Oh, so he doesn't live with his wife any more?'

Overheard on train.

'I quite fancy a massage but I couldn't stand the thought of a man rubbing me up and down.'

'Come on, who are you kidding, Christine!'

Overheard on train from Glasgow to Edinburgh. Old American lady tourist to slightly deaf Scotsman sitting opposite her.

'Excuse me, sir, but is there a rest room on this train?'

'I'm sorry, madam, but there is no restaurant on this train, but if you hold on for a couple of minutes there will be a man along with a trolley.'

Overheard on bus in Glasgow.

'Och, you do know her fine. She's quite tall and always has a hard look tae her. Looks like wan o' they bodies on *Taggart* that's been buried fur aboot six weeks.'

Overheard on bus in Motherwell.

'Did ye see the way she jist shoves food intae her mooth? It's like a wheelie bin wi' nae lid.'

Overheard on Glasgow to Edinburgh train.

'Socks with trainers look terrible. A sartorial can of worms is what I say. It's usually just fat, middle-aged men kidding themselves on.'

Overheard on easyJet flight from Glasgow to Stansted. Aircrew giving safety instructions.

'This aircraft is not being driven by Captain Sully so at least we will not land in the Hudson. But if we do land in the Irish Sea, and you are a person who is so minded, you might want to blow the wee whistle on your life jacket to attract a nice passing sailor.'

Overheard on train from Glasgow to Perth.

'She's got seven children. It's quite a big family nowadays. She's said to be very intelligent, reads library books all the time.'
'She must be a Big Issue reader.'

Overheard on bus in Kilmarnock.

'So that's us finished, eh? You're jist givin' me the heave.'
'That's it. Now you've got to admit, Sylvia, we've both had oor kick at the ba'.'
'Ah wid love tae kick yours.'

Overheard on Glasgow to Inverness train.

'You'll not believe it, he says he wants to be on the Weakest Link with that cheeky woman. Imagine going to London and making a fool of yourself like that. And his general knowledge only goes as far as reading the Sun and Celtic. I told him I can insult him any time he likes. He certainly gives me plenty of ammunition.'

Customs official inspecting passport photo at Glasgow Airport.
'Glad you're keeping better now, sir.'

Overheard on train.
'We had two nights at an hotel in St Andrews. Superb it was. The best of everything. They wait on you hand and foot. We went to a whisky tasting in the hotel. I was never too keen on whisky, even the smell of it. But I have got to say some of the malts were nice and smooth. We took a couple of bottles home and they only lasted two weeks. We need to buy some more now, and here was me brought up to be teetotal.'

Overheard on Glasgow to Edinburgh train.
'Admit it, now. It's nice tae get oot the hoose, sure it is? If it wisnae for me you would sit an' dae nothing aw day apart frae footering wi' that computer o' yours! So gie yer face a holiday an' have a wee smile.'

Overheard on Kilmarnock Dial-a-Bus.
'I found out with my kids that when they became fit to live with, they are by then living with somebody else.'

Overheard at bus stop in Cumbernauld.
'Big ideas that yin. Born tae be an executive.'
'How come?'
'Sure his fether owns half that business.'

Overheard on Peebles to West Linton bus.

'See with all this financial crisis jist noo, if ah had a job ah wid seriously consider a career change.'

Overheard on train.

'She is a slave to her kitchen. Always apron-clad, whipping up healthy purées and broccoli soup. Will die with a whisk in her hand, so she will.'

Overheard on Glasgow to Lenzie bus.

'She is noo living with that big chancer. Absolutely no manners does he have. A big ham.'

'Ye're right, an ignorant pig, he is.'

Overheard on bus.

'She says she fancies a nudist holiday in Provence. Look at her for heaven's sake. Imagine that going starkers. She would frighten the French so she would.'

Overheard on bus returning to care home after a day out at the seaside.
'Right. They're all here, driver. You can go now.'
'Aye, but all here's no' all there.'

Overheard on Clydebank bus.
'We wis fair drookit. We couldnae find a taxi anywhere. Nae umbrella either. The water wis running oot ma knickers like a plumber's nightmare.'

Overheard on train to Glasgow. Lady enters crowded compartment at Gilmour Street Station, Paisley.
'Hullorerr, Helen. How ur ye?'
'Fine, just fine. I haven't seen you around for quite a while.'
'Naw. Ah wis in Florida visitin' ma daughter. You know, the wan wi' six weans. My, that Florida is some place. Big hooses everywhere wi' swimmin' pools. Orlando is magic so it is.'
'Where does your daughter live in Florida?'
'In a big condom jist north o' Tampax.'
(Compartment in uproar. People still breaking into fits of giggles when train pulls into Glasgow Central.)

Overheard on Edinburgh to Ratho bus.
'They say you should always accept compliments graciously. I cannae do that. Anyway, ah cannae remember the last time I got one. Probably at ma wedding twenty years ago.'

Overheard at check-in desk at Glasgow Airport.
'Did you pack this yourself, sir?'
'No, ma wife packed it.'
'Where is your wife, sir?'
'At home. You can have a wee keek in the case if you like. Just don't laugh at ma string vest.'

Overheard on Largs bus going to Glasgow.
'We took the train to Mallaig. See the scenery in Scotland, well, ah wis lost for words. Then we went up to Skye. See they Cuillins wi' blue sky behind them, well, ah wis just lost for words. In fact, that week everywhere we went ah wis just lost for words.'
'Must be the first time you were ever lost for words, Marjorie.'

Overheard in check-in queue at Glasgow Airport.
'Ma son's lookin' efter the new dog while we are away. That dog is sex mad. It's screwed ma leg, ma wife's leg, and the legs o' the kitchen furniture four times. Ah'll no' be surprised if oor kitchen table has pups.'

Overheard on train at Largs.
'Now he's got himself into a right pickle. He's got a problem with his lady friend.'

'How's that?'
'Apparently his wife has found out about her.'

Overheard on bus in Edinburgh.
'I love the Sally Ann. Real good, practical Christianity ah say.
Quite prepared to go to some old woman's hoose and paint her
living room.'
'Dae ye think they would gie me an estimate!'

Overheard on bus in Montrose.
'Him! Nothin' but a misery guts. Would need a humour by-pass
tae even gie a wee smile.'

Overheard on train to Gourock from Glasgow.
'The cost o' energy is ridiculous now compared with what it used
tae be. I can remember when gas only went up when you put a
match to it.'

Overheard on Glasgow Underground.
'Sit somewhere else, would ye!'
'Not you again!'
'Aye, it sure is me.'
'How come ah'm always meeting ma pain o' an ex-wife. Ur ye
chasing efter me again?'
'Ah never chased efter you in ma life. Your mother knew ma
mother and that's how we met. You know damn well that's right.'

'Aye, an' if ah remember ma mother had bad eyesight.'
'Just listen tae it! Nae wonder ah divorced you. You're still pathetic. Never talk tae me again.'

Overheard in Buchanan Street Bus Station.
'The walls of our house are so thick you'd have to bore a hole before you would hear anything from next door.'
'Well, ma wife would be able to hear yer neighbours. She can hear wedding bells ten years doon the line.'

Overheard at bus stop in Paisley.
'I've got healthy bowels. Could set ma watch by them. Half-an-hour after ma toast ah'm sittin' there going at it.'

Overheard on bus in Anstruther. Mother addressing howling toddler.
'Look, here's that new towel ah just bought. Fur heaven's sake wrap it roon yer face an' have a good greet.'

Overheard on East Kilbride to Gogar bus.
'Blackpool always reminds me of jellied eels.'
'Ugh! Ah widnae put a jellied eel in ma mouth.'
'Prefer jelly babies, eh?'

Overheard on bus in Edinburgh.
'When the postman rang the bell he was still in the kitchen making coffee in his dressing gown.'
'The postman would be surprised. He probably makes his in a mug!'

Overheard on bus in Aberdeen.
'Not me. Ah widnae gae her a sook o' ma lolly. No' right in the head, that wan. Banjoed her man and he had tae have a wee operation in a very private place.'

Overheard on bus in Paisley.
'You forget the Rangers, ah told him. Get yersel' a good job. Rangers will no' pit a loaf oan yer table.'

Overheard on train from Paisley to Glasgow.
'Ah feel ah'm goin' tae pieces this weather. Don't seem tae cope

anymore. Ah worry aboot everything. Ah mean whit if this bird flu thing happens? Have they got a vaccine yet?'

'You've mair to worry you than bird flu, Babs. What aboot your wee problem? Ye know, in the "doonstairs" department.'

'Ah'm waiting fur a phone call tae see a doctor aboot ma "doonstairs" thingy.'

Overheard at a check-in desk at Edinburgh Airport.

'She said the best bit o' her holiday wis when she went on a gondola in Venus.'

Overheard on CityLink bus in Edinburgh.

'We went down to Downing Street but they've put security gates up since the last time I was there. Just as well. If I could have got ma hands on him I would have probably strangled him.'

Overheard on bus outside Inverness.

'No, I do my sudokus every day. Got to keep the mind active, you know. Everything else has now gone for a burton.'

Overheard on bus going to Kirkintilloch.

'See the traffic on that Kingston bridge at teatime, it's chaotic, that's whit it is.'

'Ye're right, they should just pull it doon.'

Overheard in main concourse at Glasgow Central Station.

'Will the London sleeper be called soon?'

'Listen, dearie, if it's cauld ah'll come wi' ye and warm ye up!'

Overheard in Buchanan Street Bus Station, Glasgow.

'I love going on that wee boat from Gourock pier to Helensburgh. It stops at Kilcreggan for a few minutes on the way there and on the way back. I used to love it when it was the old boat and you could sit outside and get the sea air. Now you cannae do that. You're stuck in this wee bus thing that scoots aboot the Clyde. Probably it's they daft safety regulations oot o' Brussels.'

Overheard on Flyglobespan flight from Glasgow to Majorca.
'Don't be stupid. You've had too much tae drink.'
'Ah'm fine. Look, here's the stewardess. Miss, it's been a rare smooth flight. Gonnae pass the hat roon fur the driver!'

Overheard on bus in Glasgow. Middle-aged lady, looking flummoxed, turns to passenger seated next to her.
'This is me since yesterday!'

Overheard at departure gate at Glasgow Airport.
'Not wan o' them in that care home has their wits aboot them.'
'Ah know. They've aw got that Alex Heimers.'

Overheard on train to Ayr.
'This train stops at every bloomin' station.'
'Ah wish it would stop at a lavvy. Ah'm burstin'.'

Overheard on bus in Edinburgh.

'I think the government is quite right. We should all be responsible and recycle and think green all the time.'

'I always think green.'

'Okay, give us an example, then.'

'Hibs Football Club.'

Overheard on bus in Dundee.

'My real problem is my mother. Criticises everything I do. Gives me advice on this and that. Drives me up the wall. Ah mean, ah'm in ma forties now.'

'That's a shame. Ah'm lucky. Mine's deid.'

Overheard on bus in Dundee.

'Him! Och, he sleeps like a log, so he does. It's like a sawmill going all night. The only time it stops is when he's up at the lavvy. Pity he's no' up at the lavvy mair often.'

Overheard on bus in Grangemouth.

'Ye see, she's just bought an end-terrace, semi-detached hoose.'

Overheard on bus in Brechin.

'Ah keep changing ma mind aw the time. Wan minute it's Labour, the next it's SNP. Ah've even thought of voting for the Tories.'

'You're what they call a floating voter.'

'Ah'm no' floatin', ah'm sinkin'.'

Overheard on bus in Edinburgh.

'Naw, fur me it's the Proclaimers. Ah get all emotional when ah hear their song "It's gonna be five hundred thousand million miles" an' that.'

Overheard on bus in Newton Mearns.

'But listen. I didn't do it. I've told you three times now.'

'I didn't say it was your fault, Walter. All I said was I was going to blame you.'

Overheard on train.

'Our electricity payment has just gone up again. I don't understand these energy companies. Well, I do really, all they want is our money. And we've no fireplace now. Ah blame ma partner. He got the chimney blocked off so we can't go back to coal. Even Santa cannae come noo.'

Overheard at bus stop in Port Glasgow when bus draws in.

'Excuse me, driver, is this ma bus?'

'Naw, hen, it belongs tae McGill's. But ah'll gie ye a wee hurl if you like.'

Overheard on train to Perth.
'My boyfriend's mother doesn't like me. She's quite polite but you can tell by the way she looks at me.'
'So how does she look at you?'
'As little as possible. Just a wee keek now and then.'

Overheard at bus stop in Grangemouth.
'And another thing, he leaves that loo seat up all the time. If I've told him once I've told him a million times. I blame his mother. Didnae train him and his brothers properly. And another thing.

ah couldnae believe ma ears!

He doesnae aim all that well. Says he cannae get excited aboot all this toileting stuff.'

'Well, you should just go and haud it fur him. That would fair get him straightened out!'

Overheard at platform 12, Glasgow Central Station.
'Ah see some men going aboot wi' shorts nooadays. Even if it's cauld. Ma fether would have died wi' his legs up if ye had asked him tae wear shorts. Even they funny wee hats they cyclists wear. The trouble is a lot o' men have goat better legs than women. It's no' fair is whit ah say.'

Overheard on bus in Glasgow city centre.
'An' whit aboot yer auld fether. How's the poor soul doing?'
'Ninety-six in August, so he is. Ah've just told him ah'm no' buying him ony mair green bananas.'

Overheard on bus in Edinburgh.
'You can tell by the way she dresses that all she wants to do is attract men.'
'You're so right. If you ask me she's been responsible for more merry men than Robin Hood.'

OVERHEARD DURING LEISURE ACTIVITIES

Overheard in queue at Phoenix Cinema, Linwood.
'We grew up in a tenement wi' one cludgie tae four families. See dancing aboot on a cauld landing at three o'clock in the morning waiting fur somebuddy tae finish. No joke. The wans nooadays wi' en-suites don't know they're livin', so they don't.'

Overheard in cinema queue in Dundee.
'Ah met this lovely fella the second night ah wis in Amsterdam. His English was perfect and he treated me like a lady.'
'Aye, ah heard French men are supposed tae be very romantic.'

Overheard at bingo in Kilmarnock.
'Never underestimate that wan. She might be overly daft but she's no' overly stupid.'

Overheard outside King's Theatre in Glasgow.
'I fair love they pantos. An' see when they bring down that sheet for the audience tae sing ah get aw excited an' gie it laldy. Pantos are great, sure they are?'
'Oooh no, they're not!'

Overheard at SECC in Glasgow.

'Ah like his music fine but he's a bit of a nutter noo, sure he is. Ah mean, see this business of having folks hold an umbrella over him when it's eighty degrees. See in Glesca, if it wis eighty degrees they'd aw be lying in the parks soaking it up.'

Overheard outside Pavilion Theatre in Glasgow.

'I enjoyed the show okay. But see that juggler. Kept drappin' his balls. He would need to be on the radio tae be ony good.'

Overheard at bingo in Inverclyde.

'So, how's your girl getting on, Molly?'

'Well, you know she an' her husband were havin' problems?'

'Aye, ah remember ye tellin' me.'

'Well, they've split up.'

'So, where is she staying noo?'

'She's in the same hoose. She got the hoose, the furniture an' the cat. He got the dug. Him an' that dug deserve wan another. They both stink!'

Overheard in Edinburgh Zoo.

'You see, son, people originally came from a species of ape.'

'And let me tell you, son, that's only on your father's side of the family, of course.'

Overheard at the Royal Concert Hall in Glasgow.

'Rachmaninov's Third Piano Concerto is my favourite. The finale with its ecstatic gestures makes the hair on the back of my neck rise. I just wish it would make the hair at my bald spot do the same.'

Overheard during interval at the Pavilion Theatre, Glasgow.

'Naw, naw. Ah'm no' musical in the least. Ah couldnae fart Scotland the Brave efter beans oan toast even if ye gave me a million pounds.'

Overheard as ladies dance round their handbags in a nightclub in Glasgow.
'At least naebuddy is feelin' yer bum while ye dae this.'

Overheard at art exhibition in Edinburgh.
'Wi' him an' her it's nothing but jibber-jabber aw the time.
Everybody says they just enjoy their wee fights.'

Overheard in cinema in Glasgow.
'One OAP ticket, please, for Cinema Two.'

'Have you got proof that you are sixty or over?'
'Jist clock ma dial, hen.'

Overheard in foyer of Pavilion Theatre, Glasgow
'He's let her down umpteen times. The big galoot keeps promising he will never do it again. Personally ah wouldnae trust him with ma granny's budgie.'

OVERHEARD IN HOSPITALS

Overheard in waiting room in Western Infirmary, Glasgow.
'Listen, you make any arrangements you want. Have a bloomin'
band if ye want. It's no' ma father that's died.'

Overheard in a waiting room at Southern
General Hospital, Glasgow.
'That receptionist was quite nice.
See at our local health centre the
receptionist would frighten the life
out of you. Real cheeky, she is. Ma
man says she was probably thrown
oot the Gestapo for cruelty.'

Overheard during doctor's visit to ward
in Edinburgh Royal Infirmary.
'Mrs McLaren, we have noticed orange
colours in your stools, so we will have to
keep you in for further tests.'
'Hey, haud oan a minute, doctor. Ah thought that wis jist the Irn-Bru.'

Overheard in waiting room at Glasgow Royal Infirmary.

'My cholesterol count was up at twelve before my bypass. With the statins I'm down around five. I told the wife she can put the life insurance policy back in the bureau.'

Overheard in Royal Alexandra Hospital, Paisley.

'She wis really a very selfish wumman, ye know. Only thought o' hersel', so she did. Noo she's died this morning and husnae even left oot his tea fur the night.'

Overheard in Glasgow Royal Infirmary entrance hall.

'I'm jist going in to visit oor Betty. Nice wee soul so she is. Says she might still be a spinster but she still has her dreams.'
'They must be giving her cheese at bedtime in here then.'

Overheard in Royal Alexandra Hospital, Paisley.

'I gie'd the wean a wee kiss. But ah wid have preferred tae kiss the nurse. A wee stoater she wis. That wan can take ma appendix oot ony day.'

Overheard in Edinburgh clinic.

'I'm here for a mammogram, too. I had one before and I'm not really looking forward to it. If my husband had a mammogram on his "bits and pieces" you would hear the squeals in North Berwick.'

Overheard in Glasgow Maternity Unit. Nurse talking to American lady who has just given birth, and is returning to live in the States.

'When yer wean grows up will she have a Scottish or an American accent?'

Overheard in Royal Alexandra Hospital, Paisley.

'The nurse did say that some anti-ageing creams may just turn the tide of some wrinkles on your face.'

'King Canute an' half a ton o' Botox would be needed for me.'

Overheard in Edinburgh Royal Infirmary.

'Whit a moaner. Doesnae appreciate me coming tae see him one wee bit. If he wis drowning he'd complain if it rained.'

Overheard in Ninewells Hospital, Dundee.

'I thought she looked much better today. What did you think?'

'Ah don't think she's as good as she looks. Did you know she's actually cellulite from the neck down?'

Overheard during visiting hour at a certain Scottish hospital.

'See that Posh Spice. It says in the papers she lives on five tomatoes and a handful of grapes a day. Ah couldnae dae that. Ah need fibre in ma diet or ah feel ill. Don't know how she does it.'

'Well, if she wis in here she wouldnae need five tomatoes and a handful o' grapes tae lose weight. Ah'm dying tae get oot tae get a good feed.'

Overheard in A&E at Edinburgh Royal Infirmary.
'So how did you manage to do this to yourself?'
'Well, doctor, my BMW is rear-wheel drive, and it spun out of control on black ice when I was going to work this morning.'
'Where did it happen?'
'On the slip road on to the motorway.'

Overheard at Edinburgh Royal Infirmary.
'Actually I always thought that our Jennifer would make a good nurse. She's got the right touch.'
'Depends what she's touching.'

Overheard at entrance to Inverclyde Royal Hospital.
'Hi, Charlie, are you just going home?'
'Nice tae see you, Robert. Aye, I was in having a colonoscopy.'
'Well, I'm here for an endoscopy. I hope they've given the equipment a good clean.'

Overheard in waiting room in Glasgow Royal Infirmary.
'Ah felt that depressed last night that ah nearly committed suicide.'
'So ye didnae do it, then?'

Overheard in A&E at Inverclyde Royal Hospital.
'Waitin' lang, mate?'
'About twenty minutes.'

'Whit's wrang wi' ye, mate?'
'I think I may have broken my wrist.'
'See me, mate, ah've drank too much o' that Fairy Liquid, mate.'

Overheard in a waiting room at Glasgow Royal Infirmary.
'No, I'm up about six times a night, standing there with nothing coming out. It's very frustrating and annoying if I wake the wife. She calls me her "cannae wee man".'

Overheard in waiting room at Tom Weldon Building, Gartnavel Hospital, Glasgow.
'Ah've taken anti-depressant tablets noo for fifteen years, an' ah've went tae they group psychology sessions. Nane o' it seems tae work. It wid make ye mad so it wid. And see ma man, he's that cheery aw the time. Ye wid think he would at least have some consideration for ma condition.'

Overheard in foyer of a Glasgow hospital.
'Ma operation was cancelled at the last minute. They couldnae get an anaesthetist.'
'If ah'd known, ah wid have come in and given you the old "one-two".'

Overheard in waiting room at Edinburgh Royal Infirmary.
'I don't know why I'm here for this examination. Ma wife says all ah need is a rub-down wi' rough sandpaper tae take the edge aff me.'

Overheard outside the ladies' loo in Aberdeen hospital.
'She's been in that lavvy fur ten minutes. Ah mean, sure aw you've got tae dae is pull yer knickers doon an get oan wi' it!'

Overheard in foyer of Glasgow Royal Infirmary.
'I heard he wis a bit off colour yesterday. How is he noo?'
'Deid!'

Overheard in waiting room of Falkirk and District Royal Infirmary.

'I just cannae get into a book. A couple of chapters and that's me. I much prefer magazines.'
'I'm the very opposite. Read all the time, I do. Probably at least two a week. Every spare minute I've got my nose in a book.'
'I prefer a hankie.'

Overheard in Gartnavel Hospital, Glasgow.
'She asked for a bedpan and it took twenty minutes before it came. Well, wi' her bowels you can imagine whit happened.'

Overheard in ward at Southern General Hospital, Glasgow.
'Are these Paisley print pyjamas yours, Mister Lewis?'
'Ah usually sleep in the scuddy, nurse. Ah wouldnae be seen dead in these.'
'Well, Mister Lewis, when ma father died they found fifty pounds in his pyjama pocket.'
'Give me the fifty quid an' ah'll wear them, nurse.'

Overheard in waiting room at Aberdeen Infirmary.
'I've got to the stage, so I have, well I am sixty-eight, that if I get a new pain it takes a couple o' days before I can get around to worrying about it alang wi' aw the rest.'

Overheard in ward at Western Infirmary, Glasgow.
'I don't know about you but ah'm sweating. It's that hot in here.'
'It's the heat that's doing it.'

Overheard in maternity reception area at Royal Alexandra Hospital, Paisley. Granny talking to receptionist.
'Ah wis giving birth tae oor Kenneth when the news o' Kennedy's assassination came through. It came intae ma mind again when ah wis birthin' oor Pauline, as there wis nae news that day.'

Overheard in waiting room in Royal Alexandra Hospital, Paisley.

'Drugs seem tae be everywhere noo. There's a family in the next street tae us who are all intae drugs.'

'The whole family? How many are there?'

'A single mother and four teenagers. Apparently they are on absolutely everything. Anything they can get their hands on. Ah wis told that wan o' the boys is even addicted tae brake oil.'

'Don't tell me. He says he can stop any time he wants to, eh?'

OVERHEARD AT THE GYM

Overheard at Scottish Slimmers in Glasgow.
'For all my bulk I'm actually quite a light eater.'
'Aye, as soon as it's light ye start eatin'! Good job it gets dark at night.'

Overheard at a gym in Paisley.
'Ye're better trying to lose weight gradually and being sensible about what you eat. See these women that go in for this liposuction, if they take away too much fat it will cost them a fortune in new knickers.'

Overheard at a ladies' weekly aerobics session.
'Ah love they Jaffa Cakes. Eat aboot three a day. No' really fattening and they certainly keep me regular.'

Overheard at spinning class in Glasgow.
'She might have lost three stones but ah can tell ye she's still a wee scrubber. She was a wee fat scrubber at school, tae. Never improved hersel'. Says mair than her prayers so she does.'

Overheard at slimming club in Port Glasgow.
'Do you weigh at home?'
'We've got an' auld set o' scales in the bathroom. They're no' accurate, though. Ma partner says he's going tae get me a new set. Wan where there's a thing on it you can adjust. A setting that tells you stones and pounds, a setting that just tells you pounds, a setting that tells you kilograms, an' a setting that just tells you lies!'

Overheard at fitness centre in Saltcoats.
'Ah never weigh masel' until efter ah've had a whoopsie.'

Overheard at slimming club in Paisley.
'I've got to hide any selection boxes that come into the house. My John's a chocoholic. You just can't trust him. One Mars bar and he's away.'

Overheard at WeightWatchers in Paisley.
'You know all this business about inside everybody there is a thin person struggling to get out? Well, I can usually sedate my thin person with a couple of packets of salt and vinegar crisps.'

Overheard at weight-loss club in Greenock.
'Her weight see-saws aw the time. Up an' doon, up an' doon, like the weather. She should go tae a gym as well as this club instead o' goin' fur kerry-oots every night.'

Overheard at slimming club in Glasgow.
'It is not just losing weight that improves you. I think the key item is your hair. I tried to get an appointment for today but it looks like it'll need tae be Friday. Ah mean it's like straw hingin' oot a midden, sure it is.'

Overheard at a gym in Paisley.
'Slimming is fine but I felt that I had to do something else as well. So I took up yoga about three months ago. I feel it has improved my posture and pulled my tummy in. And I can now almost put my legs behind my head.'
'That'll be handy if you want to scratch your ears.'

Overheard at a gym reception. Manager talking to member.
'So, Jasmina, next week we'll try out some exercises. Just light stuff. How flexible are you?'
'Well, ah cannae make Wednesdays or Thursdays.'

Overheard at an induction talk by health club manager.
'I have got to tell you, ladies, that as you age your skin gets older.'

Overheard at Scottish Slimmers.

'He is a bit o' a ladies' man. Ah wis warned about him when we met up. Now ah've found out he doesnae have ony heart, just one big slimy, swinging brick.'

Overheard in a fitness centre's changing room in Ayr.

'Actually all this slimming business is a racket. It's nothing but a load o' mince.'

'Oh, mince. Good idea. I think I'll make him mince and tatties for his tea.'

Overheard at ladies' exercise class in Glasgow.

'Now, get yer bahookies moving up. … Did ye no' hear me? Get yer erses higher!'

OVERHEARD IN THE PUB

Overheard in pub in Callander.

'Och, you do know him. Lives oot on the Stirling Road. Always wears a bunnet. Has a face like Ken Dodd's granny's uncle.'

Overheard in pub in Edinburgh.

'You're a right wee cracker, so ye are.'

'Aye, well, ye can forget aboot pullin' me.'

Overheard in pub in Dunoon.

'They should have a quiz in Dunoon called, "Find somebody sober at our Highland Games". Naebuddy would win a prize.'

Overheard in pub in Linwood.

'They say that wives are rational and understanding only in direct proportion to the distance frae their mothers.'

'Tell me aboot it. Ma wife phones her mother three times a day, an' she only lives four hooses away.'

Overheard in pub in Airdrie.
'Sorry, but ye cannae smoke in here. All pubs are now non-smoking.'
'Ah bet ye they didnae have ony non-smoking lifeboats on
the Titanic.'
'Aye, an' they didnae have ony lavvies on the lifeboats either, even
though they were aw shittin' themselves.'

Overheard in pub in Edinburgh.
'Inspiration! Don't talk to me about inspiration. I've been
inspired aw ma life tae do this and that, and it's got me
naewhere. In future ah'll just stick tae constipation!'

Overheard in pub in Glasgow.
'Watch yersel' wi' that wan o'er there. He's goat the manners o' a
seagull eating crusts an' dirty nappies.'

Overheard at pub quiz in Aberdeen.
'Those of you at the back who can't hear me, please put your
hands up.'

Overheard in pub in Greenock.
'It's no' ma ideal job, but a job's a job nooadays. Better than a slap
on the kisser wi' a wet haddie is whit ah say.'

Overheard in pub in Glasgow.
'He's got an allotment somewhere behind the motorway. Always

up there. Grows his own vegetables and stuff. Says it gies him exercise and saves money. Ma wife's a rerr terr. Says he's a bit o' a turnip himsel'.'

Overheard in pub in Glasgow.
'And how's your father?'
'Still deid.'

Overheard in pub in Edinburgh.
'If you hang in there for years and years and really get quite old, then your various wee parts get quite interesting.'

Overheard in hotel bar in Glasgow.
'Cannae hold his liquor, him. Two or three and he's legless. As far as he's concerned an ice lolly is a stiff drink.'

Overheard in pub in Glasgow.
'Ah always say ma favourite drink is the next wan.'

Overheard in pub in Glasgow.
'What dae ye think aboot them keepin' a national DNA database, eh? Mind you it might keep crime doon if aw the villains knew they would be caught.'
'Ah'm no' sure ah fancy ma DNA being kept.'

'Are you gonnae commit a crime, then?'
'The only crime ah ever committed wis marrying your sister.'

Overheard in pub in Dunoon.
'Noo he thinks he might become a driving instructor. He saw an advert saying that no previous experience was required. It's a bit of a worry that. At the moment he only has a provisional. But if he wants tae do it ah'll no' stand in his way.'

Overheard in pub in Aberdeen.
'He's got some lifestyle. Works oot in Dubai for three months then hame fur a fortnight. Then back oot tae the sun. Ah widnae fancy it masel'. Wid miss the dart matches an' that though.'

Overheard in pub in Glasgow.
'He can play the ukulele tae.'
'Clever fella.'
'Started aff on the guitar. But apparently the ukulele is more difficult.'
'Ah widnae know. Ma family wisnae musical. Mind you, once at a family party ma fether played a tune using lemonade bottles filled with water. Then he did an encore wi' a comb and toilet paper.'
'The mind boggles!'

Overheard in pub in Edinburgh.
'It's all this political correctness nowadays. You wouldn't have

got that with Harold Wilson. A shrewd wee man that.
Underrated he wis. Nane o' this Brussels stuff wi him.'

Overheard in hotel lounge in Crieff.
'Did you know that crime rates apparently go up when there is a full moon. Mind you, I never see much crime around here. What do you think?'
'Well, occasionally. Probably once in a blue moon.'

Overheard in Edinburgh pub.
'I can't be bothered with fancy foods any more. I just like the simple stuff. A pie and a pint is meat and drink tae me.'

Overheard in pub in Glasgow.
'No, I just take Alka-Seltzer in the morning if it's been a heavy night on the bevvy. Makes me good as new.'
'No hangover, then?'
'Och, just a wee headache and maybe feeling a bit rough for a few hours.'

Overheard at karaoke in pub in Edinburgh.
'Naw, ah cannae sing.'
'Everybody can sing, missus.'
'Aye, the burds.'
'You're a burd.'
'Aye, an auld wan wi' a pension.'

Overheard in pub in Airdrie.
'He is absolutely loaded, so he is, and here's me skint. He drives wan o' they big gas-guzzlers. Ma trouble is, ye see, ah'm a beer guzzler.'

Overheard in hotel bar in Pitlochry.
'It is really a fine point about when life itself actually begins.'
'As far as I'm concerned it starts with the first whisky of the day.'

Overheard in club bar in Bathgate.
'This generation is brainwashed into believing that a pint will kill you. Absolute nonsense. Ma father had a couple o' pints most nights and a few more at the weekend and it didnae kill him.'
'So how old wis he when he died?'
'Fifty-two. But that wis because he wis run over by the works bus.'

Overheard in pub in Bathgate.
'She's been in the huff all day. I was glad to get out. Just gives me dirty looks but says nothing. I've even apologised to get her out of it, even although it wasn't my fault. My mother warned me about her. Apparently her mother was aye huffy, tae.'

Overheard in pub in Edinburgh.

'I could have had a heart attack at any time. It wis that bad. I wis just lucky I had a blood sample taken because of my haemorrhoids.'

Overheard in pub in Paisley.

'See they saving and mortgage rates, they go up an' doon like a hoor's knickers, so they do.'

Overheard in pub in Edinburgh.

'So, why did ye move fae Glesca tae Edinburgh in the first place?'
'Fur work. Whit did ye think it wis fur? The Witness Protection Programme?!'

Overheard in bar in Alloa.

'Ah'll have a pint o' yer best an' ma wife wull have a sweet sherry.'
'Oh, right. Can ye jist remind me whit ah have tae pit in it tae make it sweet?'

OVERHEARD OUT AND ABOUT

Overheard outside church in Kilmacolm.
'Well, did you enjoy visiting the church, dear? What did you think of the new stained-glass windows?'
'They were very nice, Grandpa, but I didn't see God. But I think I heard him hoovering in the hall.'

Overheard in swimming pool in Glasgow.
'My husband was just about to go out the door when ah shouted

tae him that the baby was coming. Fifteen minutes later there was the baby all delivered. I have got to say he was a great help but now he thinks there's nothing tae having a baby. Thinks he's great. Tellin' all his pals. If he wis chocolate he would eat himsel'.'

Overheard in queue at Job Centre in Edinburgh.
'Ma wife used tae call me Bob the Builder fur a joke. Since being made redundant and scouting around for a job, she now calls me Bob-a-Job.'

Overheard in room in care home. Old lady who had just moved in being visited by her niece.
'Nice room and lovely view, Auntie.'
'Yes, and I have everything I need in here.'
'What do you do if you want to contact somebody?'
'Oh, we have intercourse in every room.'

Overheard in care home. Two care attendants talking.
'When I answered his buzzer there he wis in the bare scuddy, the light shining aff his glass eye. So I got his dressing goon on him heap pronto, and said to him, "Listen, Mister Harris, whit would the Care Commission say if they saw you like this? You're a naughty boy, you know." So he just says, "I would like to be a naughty boy." Let me tell you from what I could see it's been a long time since that one wis capable o' being a naughty boy.'

Overheard at wedding service in Perth. Little boy with loud voice, whose mummy had told him the previous week about the birds and the bees whilst emphasising it was only for married people.

'I now pronounce you man and wife.'

'Does he give her the seed now, Mummy?'

Overheard in public toilet in Glasgow.

'She might have lost a stone but she is still flabby in bits. What she really needs is a good, firm bra. Somebody should really tell her. It's like two puppies fighting under a blanket.'

Overheard in vet's waiting room in Perth.

'What a lovely, wee puppy.'

'Thanks. He's a miniature German Schnauzer. Unfortunately he has a bit of a temperature.'

'What you would call a wee German hotdog, eh?'

Overheard beside a field of newborn lambs near Galashiels. Farmer stapling yellow disk on each lamb's ear.

'Look, Dad, they've left the price tags on the sheep.'

Overheard in hotel in Edinburgh.

'I absolutely detest people belittling others. Gossip and vindictiveness are not nice attributes to have.'

'You are quite correct. When I think on Lily MacIntosh that you and I went to school with. There's an example of someone who is always talking about others.'

'I remember Lily MacIntosh very well. She was nearly expelled for writing love letters to the French teacher. Bit of a nutcase, if I remember. And I hear she gets all her clothes out of charity shops.'

Overheard at nightclass in Kilmarnock.
'Ah cannae stop writing ma name wi' his surname. Dae ye think that proves ah'm in love wi' him?'

'Probably just proves you're nae good at spelling!'

Overheard during Ramblers' Club outing.
'Funnily enough ah once knew a Nobbie, an' he had nobbly knees, too.'

Overheard at Hogmanay party in Glasgow.
'I only make New Year resolutions that can be broken by the second of January. Saves you a lot of worry so it does.'

Overheard at wedding reception.
'Look at that dress, isn't it just lovely? And she's had hersel' made up by a beautician. Isn't she stunning?'

'Aye, an' look at the groom. He looks stunned as well.'

158   ah couldnae believe ma ears!

Overheard in care home in Lanark.
'I love all these Personal adverts in the paper.'
'Oh, so do I. But I'm too old now to apply.'
'Don't you believe it. There was one recently which said
"Vivacious seventy-five-year-old looking for man with
comfortable car." Some folks have got a cheek. Probably looking
for someone to push her wheelchair.'

Overheard at Edinburgh Hogmanay street party.
'No, Gordon didn't come. Just sits in front of the old goggle box
all the time. If anybody gets their money's worth out the licence
fee it's him. Just sits there flicking through the channels. You
start watching a programme and the next thing he's on to
another one in a flash. I think I'll start calling him Flash
Gordon.'

Overheard at Falkirk Wheel.
'Since you took these two paracetamol do you feel better, worse
or just the same?'
'Aye.'

Overheard in Argyll country house hotel. Young lad being interviewed for
general duties.
'And how is your punctuality?'
'Ach, I've nae time for aw thae commas an' things.'

Overheard in Perth hotel.

'My father had a poacher's pocket in his overcoat. Never ever had a rabbit or a salmon in it though. Only half-bottles of whisky.'

Overheard in church in Gourock.

'See all this recession business. Some people are still living off the fat o' the land. See me, ah'm carrying it around.'

Overheard in Oban.

'I didn't realise that some of the Scottish islands have no trees whatsoever. What do the poor dogs do, eh?'

Overheard in Aviemore town centre.
'Hello there, Margaret. I'm afraid I've got a wee bit of upsetting news to give you.'
'Oh. Is it good or bad?'

Overheard outside house in Stirling at Hogmanay.
'Ah love the bells at Hogmanay. Makes me think of ma mither's clootie dumplin'. Dae ye remember they wee china dolls, bachelors' buttons and silver threepennies they put in them. Wance ma wee sister swallowed a button and we had tae take her tae the hospital. It wis great fun.'

Overheard in Dingwall.
'Me an' him is fine. It's just occasionally we have a wee ding-dong. It's usually aboot his mother. Thank God she's away noo. But see when we're no' fightin' we get on smashin'.'

Overheard in Oban.
'People eat far too much. See that cake there. It could feed a family o' four for six months and hauf the population o' Skye for a fortnight.'

Overheard in hotel in Crieff.
'She's the type that never sees ordinary doctors, it's always a consultant or a senior consultant. Always talks about going to see "my consultant". Gie ye the boke it would.'

Overheard near garden centre in Inverness.

'We were just in there looking at lawnmowers. And my "technical genius" here asks the assistant how do you start it? So the assistant said all you need is a big jerk on the cord. Well, ah nearly wet masel' laughing.'

OVERHEARD IN THE BANK

Overheard in Bank of Scotland in Paisley.

'Teller number four.'

'Teller number one.'

'Teller number three.'

'On you go. You're next.'

'Naw, ah'm waitin' for teller number five.'

'Does he give you mair money, then?'

'Naw, but he's very nice. Cheers me up. Always asks if I want a loan or a mortgage, and here's me nearly eighty.'

Overheard in Bank of Scotland in Stirling.

'Ah couldnae stay in the hoose aw day. Ah've goat tae get oot even if it's pissin' doon. Ah just jump oan a bus and intae the toon. Then back fur Countdown. Ah loved that Richard Whiteley. Ah wis heartbroken when he died. A real gentleman he wis.'

Overheard in Nationwide in Glasgow.

'They're back and in their new house. She said they had missed the family. They had bought a flat on the Costa del Sol but just couldn't settle. She said it was like staying in a foreign country.'

Overheard in Royal Bank of Scotland in Edinburgh.

'Oh, hello there, Tom. Haven't seen you around for a while. You been away?'

'No, I haven't been anywhere, but anyways I'm back now.'

Overheard in Bank of Scotland in Airdrie.

'Ye cannae trust anybuddy these days. See these bank managers! The debt they've got this country into. Ma man uses a word fur them that rhymes wi' bankers!'

Overheard in Clydesdale in Dundee.

'Nice couple. Always out together. Recently renewed their vows in the church. Ah couldnae dae that, ye ken. Sometimes when he is sittin' there snoring in his chair ah wish ah wis single again.'

'Don't be daft. Ye're in yer seventies.'

Overheard in Bank of Scotland, Greenock. Two men talking.

'See banks, ah've lost faith in them. The only bank ah wid deposit in noo is a sperm bank.'

'Aye, and once you'd made your deposit you'd probably lose interest!'

Overheard in Bank of Scotland in Ayr.
'Ah don't mind an ugly man as long as he doesnae smoke.
Smokin' gets up ma nose, so it does.'

Overheard in Yorkshire Building Society in Edinburgh.
'Now don't interrupt, Jean, but I'm going to ask the cashier a daft
question.'
'Huh! Believe me, you can ask daft questions better than
anybody I know.'

Overheard in Royal Bank in Glasgow.
'Money and me just don't get on. I've had premium bonds for
over twenty years and won absolutely nought. Ah think ye may
as well pit yer money in the lottery. At least ye occasionally get a
tenner back. Sure life's just wan big gamble, sure it is.'

Overheard in Bank of Scotland in Kilmarnock.
'Oh, hello, Margaret. My, you're looking so much better and
brighter than the last time ah saw you. You looked a bit tired and
yer face wis a bit yellow.'
'Thanks, Hazel. I've got to say I'm feeling so much better. It's the
new tablets I got from the doctor. I forget what you call them.
Impro— something or other. Anyway, I certainly feel they've
taken five years off ma life.'

OVERHEARD AT FUNERALS

Overheard in Co-operative Undertaker's premises before the service.

'Sorry, sur, but ye cannae smoke in here.'

'Ah havnae lit up. Ah'm just holding it.'

'No smoking on these premises, sur. It's against the law and disrespectful to the deceased.'

'Ah told ye, ah huvnae lit up yet. Anyways, he wis ma uncle and loved a wee puff himsel'.'

Overheard at a certain crematorium in the West of Scotland. Crematorium assistant talking to friend who is attending a funeral.

'No, we've a busy day today. We've got ten runners and riders.'

Overheard outside Linn Crematorium in Glasgow.

'That's some cough you've got. Ah heard it during the service.'

'Tell me about it. Ah cannae seem tae get rid of it. Had it for weeks. Been through umpteen bottles of cough mixture and

fourteen million packets of Fisherman's Friend.'
'Have you not seen your doctor?'
'Him! Couldnae cure a herring!'

Overheard during funeral tea in Paisley.
'What amazes me is that at funeral teas nobody ever talks about the deceased. By the way, how did the Gers get on last night?'

Overheard outside church following funeral service.
'I love that Latin requiem. That bit about the joy that awaits you in the afterlife, it's wonderful. When you hear it you cannae wait to get there.'
'Talk fur yersel'.'

Overheard at Falkirk Crematorium. Large number of mourners waiting to enter the sanctuary. Assistant minister trying to help.
'Don't worry. We'll get you all in. The more the merrier.'

Overheard at funeral tea in Greenock.
'Cheers. Ah like tae unwind wi a wee drink when ah go hame at night, tae. In fact ah fairly look forward tae ma sherry. Ye need a wee thing tae look forward tae during the day, sure ye do.'

Overheard after funeral service in church in Greenock.
'No, he's going to be buried at Knocksnairhill Cemetery way up on the hill. He didn't have a good view from his house and he always said he wanted a view of the Clyde.'

Overheard outside hall after funeral tea.
'Lovely purvey. Sure it wis, Jessie. Plenty o' chips an' stuff.'

Overheard outside crematorium in Glasgow. Old lady talking to friend.
'Ma friends keep dying on me. Ah think ah'll need tae get a season ticket for this place. Ah don't really mind coming here as long as it's not in a starring role.'

Overheard at funeral service.
'See her, second row in. The one with the greyish hat. Well, she's a widow hersel' noo. A couple o' year ago her husband wis fatally killed by a train.'

Overheard in crematorium in Edinburgh.
'Funnily enough, all my life I've had this lifelong ambition to be an undertaker.'
'You're on your own there, pal!'

OVERHEARD AT THE SCHOOL GATES

Overheard outside school in Erskine.

'I remember the sort of gastronomic endurance tests we had to suffer for school dinners. Jam Roly Poly or that white muck wi wee dots in it. Wouldnae gie it tae ma cat, and she died twenty years ago.'

Overheard outside school in Edinburgh.

'So he just gave him a piece of his mind. Went his dinger, so to speak.'

'And what did wee Peter do?'

'He didn't say anything. He just gave Andrew a piece of his fist.'

Overheard outside school in Paisley.

'My father is a lollipop man at a school in Glasgow. We used tae kid him on he only liked it because you didnae need tae start work till ye were sixty-five. He always has the same wee joke. Says ye cannae lick being a lollipop man.'

Overheard outside school gate in Dundee.
'Stop sniffin', you.'
'Ah've nae hankie.'
'Ah gi'ed ye wan yesterday.'
'But there wis nae paper in the school lavvy, mammy.'

Overheard at school gate in Crieff.
'He still believes in Santa. Thinks that Rudolph ate the carrots he left under the Christmas tree. It was me that had to eat them, and would you believe it cost me a filling.'

Overheard at school gate in Glasgow.
'We had a laugh with Charlie's prayers last night. I told him to pray for Samantha who is off school at present with chickenpox. So, he said, "Dear God, Samantha is not well, but I don't like her anyway." '

Overheard outside school gate in Glasgow.
'He is really a dirty, wee midden. Ah cannae seem tae get through tae him the importance of hygiene. Sometimes ah feel like wringing his neck, but it would need a good scrub first.'

Overheard at school gate in Dundee.
'See all this business of assisted suicide,

well our Martin says he's got a pile o' teachers he'd like to help. Mind you ah can think of a few folks masel'.'

Overheard outside school gate in Bathgate.
'Maths wis never ma strong point. Algebra is still a mystery tae me to this day. Some folk just loved it. Never yet found whit good it wis tae ye when ye left the school. I used tae think it wis perhaps used in Algeria.'

Overheard at school gate in Edinburgh. Mum picking up five-year-old.
'Mummy, will there be any plonkers on the road today?'

Overheard as teacher took details from mother of new pupil being admitted to school.
'Pupil's name, please?'
'Madonna.'
'Date of birth?'
'First of February, two thousand and four.'
'Name of mother?'
'That's me. Margaret.'
'Name of father?'
'Aye, well, noo yer askin', urn't ye!'

Overheard outside school in Falkirk.
'Brian didn't do very well in that exam. Most unusual. He was mad at himself for making so many wrong mistakes.'

Overheard at the school gate in Port Glasgow.
'I caught him showing his wee-wee to the wee lassie next door. My partner says he just likes to show off. Heaven knows what he will be like when he grows up.'

Overheard at school gate in Bathgate.
'So how is your eldest son getting on. Is he working now?'
'Yes, he seems to be doing quite well for such a young lad. He is an insurance claim adviser. Been doing it for two months now.'
'That must be interesting. What does he deal with?'
'Mostly car accident claims.'
'Did he take a crash course, then?'

Overheard outside school gate in Linlithgow.
'Kevin tells me that he is going to be one of the donkeys in the school nativity play in a fortnight. My husband said to him as long as it's not one of the donkeys I backed at Ayr last week. Kevin didnae get the joke, and said, "No, Dad, there will be two donkeys and Archie and I are in one of the costumes. I'm at the front." So my husband asks him how we will recognise which donkey he will be in and our Kevin says, "Sure I will be wearing my glasses, Dad."'

Overheard at school gate in Ayr.
'See this business of having boys learn tae knit in school, it's nonsense. Fine fur the girls but how many boys are gonnae thank ye fur learnin' them. Their pals will take a rise oot o' them. It's all this political correctness gone mad. Ah bet the school cannae get its budget unless it fits knittin' intae the curriculum or somethin'. The hale thing is nothing but a stitch-up if you ask me.'

Overheard at school gate in Aberdeen.
'I was no good at spelling at the school. "Chrysanthemum" is a terrible word tae spell, impossible fur the likes o' me. And I always say that "shit" was only invented because nobody could spell "diarrhoea".'

Overheard at school gate in Glasgow.
'So I just told him to sit on the naughty step. He can just twist me round his wee finger so he can, but sometimes he goes too far. Sits there with a wee tear in his eye. It brings a wee tear to my eye, too. But you've got to do it.'
'Well, ah just gie mine a couple of slaps on the bum. And efter ah've slapped their bum there's nae chance of them sittin' on any naughty step.'

Overheard at school gate in Greenock. Grandpa collecting five-year-old.
'Sorry, but I've forgotten the booster seat.'

'That's okay, Grandpa. Just get out your laptop and order one online.'

Overheard at school gate in Newton Mearns.
'Hello, Isabella. Did you have a good day at school?'
'Yes, Mum.'
'So what did you tell the teacher today for your oral diary?'
'I told the teacher we got a new television out of Currys and we are paying it up at nineteen pounds a month.'
'Ohh...!'

Overheard at school gate in Airdrie.
'I think you are telling me a wee fib, James Duff!'
'I am. But you've got to admit it's a good wee fib, Mum.'